Dear London

Irma Kurtz writes a regular column for
Cosmopolitan. Her most recent books are *The Great
American Bus Ride* (Fourth Estate, 1994) and *Irma
Kurtz's Ten-Point Plan*. She was born in Jersey
City, and is a graduate of Columbia University.
She lives in Soho.

Dear London

Notes from the Big City

IRMA KURTZ

FOURTH ESTATE ● *London*

This paperback edition published in 1998

First published in Great Britain in 1997 by
Fourth Estate Limited
6 Salem Road
London W2 4BU

Copyright © 1997 by Irma Kurtz

1 3 5 7 9 10 8 6 4 2

The right of Irma Kurtz to be identified as the author
of this work has been asserted by her in accordance with the
Copyright, Designs and Patents Act 1988.

A catalogue record for this book is available from
the British Library.

ISBN 1-85702-674-8

All rights reserved. No part of this publication may be
reproduced, transmitted, or stored in a retrieval system, in any
form or by any means, without permission in writing from
Fourth Estate Limited.

Typeset by MATS
Southend-on-Sea, Essex
Printed in Great Britain by
Clays Ltd, St. Ives plc
Bungay, Suffolk

*To my American brother, Michael,
and my English son, Marc: here and there.*

Contents

Dear London

Marble Arch

'It would have to happen on a Sunday, wouldn't it?' I said, explaining myself as usual to the driver before the taxi door had closed behind me.

'Sod's law, innit?' he replied automatically, not bothered to know what I was talking about, more concerned to see another taxi safely past on the outside before we pulled away. London taxi drivers extend courtesies to fellow cabbies that they'd rather fight than offer a civilian, especially if the poor jerk happens to be driving a Volvo. After 30 years of back-seat exchanges I'm still not absolutely sure why London cabbies among their many shared idiosyncrasies hold a pathological antipathy to people who drive Volvos: the explanation could be anything from reverse snobbery to Volvo's homonymous near-miss to female genitalia.

Witlessly my tongue returned to the cavern in a molar, top left, where a filling had departed the day before taking along part of the tooth.

'My wife can't get me to the dentist,' the taxi driver said, working up a little interest for me. His wedding ring slid on his left hand when he turned the wheel and there was an unsettled pause before the word 'wife'.

'Most men are afraid of dentists,' I said. 'It's one of those fears men don't mind talking about.'

'Like spiders,' he said. 'There's no shame in it for a bloke.'

I've never been afraid of the dentist. My father was a dentist. Of course I would have preferred him to be something posh – a violinist say, or a criminal lawyer – but even though he infuriated me and mortified me throughout my youth, our love was deep, and I cannot say he ever frightened me. There was not the slightest threat, not at the worst of times, he would desert me and what other reason can there be in the normal course of things for a girl to fear her father? Besides, Americans are raised to trust dentists in general and to have faith that their own are the best in the world. The day a Yankee like me finally entrusts her pearly-whites to a dentist of another nation, that's the day she becomes something more than a tourist. The first time I rinsed and spat for Mr Rabin of Kendal Street, on the instant my clove-tinged blood entered London's sewage, I became a bona fide turntooth on the road to expatriation. He took over where dad left off half my life ago. At least Mr Rabin is a Jew, or so I assume: I sometimes still even after all these years in England mistake a Welshman for a Jew.

Settling back into a London black taxi is to feel immediately elegant and composed, even when merely bound for an appointment with the dentist. For a start it's grand to know that the man behind the wheel is a professional and not an electrical engineer fresh off the plane from Odessa like so many of his counterparts in New York or Los Angeles. Not only is the London driver a skilled chauffeur for hire, he is curator of a venerable collection of city streets with long literary and historical connections. Before he qualified, he had to spend a year or two on a moped, 'doing the knowledge' they call it, taking in the terrain of London inch by inch. Peel a London cabbie and under his skin will be revealed the whole vast metropolitan tangle, and not just the inner workings of the city or the tourist attractions. Acton, Hornsey, Hackney, Lewisham, Bow, and all the other boroughs are technically and spiritually part of the city's nervous system and whether a cabbie likes it or not he must take them to heart too, for he's duty-bound to deliver passengers into them, even on rainy Saturday nights from the theatre district when he'd much rather not. Far-flung London has a peculiarly suburban urban ethos which is unique among capital cities. Only a stone's throw from the banks and offices of the main streets commuters on their way to the Northern Line stop at a local shop to pick up fertiliser for their roses. On any summer evening great numbers of genuine Londoners can be found killing slugs in their gardens.

With no trace of an older husband's restraint, my driver swivelled so he could watch a pretty girl in a mini-skirt who was crossing at the light, flashing her thighs in the thin sun of early May. The average Londoner needs very little encouragement, no more than one skittish ray through the clouds will do, and he or she immediately tears off clothes, then hurls the sun-starved body down on any nearby open space. In the 1960s when I'd been living in London for just under a year, I was riding on top of the number 19 bus one morning on my way to work, and as we were pulling up to Hyde Park Corner a big tree in bud brushed the window next to me. Hanging high in its branches like male and female cocos de mer of tropical islands were a tightly-furled umbrella and a bowler hat. Further articles of male apparel lay on the grass below and standing a few paces away from the trunk of the tree I saw a middle-aged man, stark naked and exultant. His head was tilted back, his pale arms were stretched wide as if to embrace the sun and he was up to his bare ass in early daffodils. I looked around at my fellow passengers. A young woman across the aisle winked at me; nobody else was paying him the slightest bit of attention.

My driver slid the window between us open wider.

'Open wide,' I thought.

'Is it painful?' he asked.

'The tooth?' I sighed inwardly.

My son's theory is that a democratic gene drives all us Americans willy-nilly to put on a semblance of egalitarian mateyness everywhere we go and regardless of how hateful and shirty we may actually be feeling. Marc himself was born in

London of an English father and has escaped the gregarious imperative of his maternal side. My sweet boy is too shy, too courteous, too conscious of every free man's right to privacy, and yes he's a little too superior too – altogether too *English* – to treat bus queues as potential seminars for consciousness raising, the way his mother does. He keeps telling me: 'Not to worry, mum'; it's probably not my fault, and maybe he's right, maybe the trait is genetically imprinted and my American garrulity is hereditary. Or maybe it's the old irritating, life-saving Jewish paranoia that compels me in spite of myself to charm every blessed soul who crosses my path. When I find myself in an enclosed space of any kind with anyone, anyone at all, *not* befriending him or her or them makes me anxious and uncomfortable. I am remorselessly outgoing, whatever the reason: I wouldn't be surprised if it is simply that having in the end spent most of my life alone, somewhere along the line silence became too intimate to share with strangers.

'Oh no. Not really painful,' I said, longing for peace and quiet, cursing my talkative genes. 'No. No. On Sunday morning there I was reading my papers, you know, and a back molar broke, crack! In half. Just like that. Out of the blue. No. No pain, not really.'

No pain. Only sharp twinges of regret that I had so heedlessly become old and dry and frangible. *Phoned in a lie the French found easy to crack* (9): 'Phoned' = rang; 'French' opening 'fr'; 'lie' = odd bits; the whole lot = 'easy to crack', or *frangible* as an old broad's molar.

English crosswords hurt, like breaking in new shoes. I lived in Paris for barely a year before I spoke French a lot better than I will ever speak *Times* crossword. The brain needs four or five days of practice every week for months before it begins to conform to the low poetry of the métier. Not that I try every day or even very often to wiggle into the cast of a puzzle-setter's mind and adapt to his awful puns and anagrams and mealy-mouthed classical references. About twelve years ago I knew an Englishman who used to get out of bed an hour earlier than he had to so he could study *The Times* crossword carefully and slowly over morning tea, referring often to the *OED* and *Brewer's Dictionary of Phrase and Fable*. When he had most of the answers by heart, he'd wait until we were on the train to fill them in where his performance attracted covert glances of admiration and envy. That gloriously disguised nitwit, by the by, was the Last of My Great Loves.

From where I'd picked up the taxi in Soho to Marble Arch looks a straightforward journey on the map. But there's no destination in London that cannot be approached by a variety of routes. My driver decided to take Oxford Street where pedestrians are as heel-to-toe as on any major avenue in New York, lots of them foreign visitors obeying their own merry down-home rules of the pavement. The French scamper talking constantly, Italian students weave four abreast and stick together through thick and thin; Spanish-speaking men are preceded by their women into hazardous terrain; Americans, glued to their maps, stop to confer at every corner, except the New Yorkers – you can always tell them by the way they edge forward into the gutter to be off their marks the instant the light changes in their favour. As for the locals, older Londoners walk pretty much as they drive, irresolute and ready at the first chance to fall into a sloppy column; only young men make it a point to cross streets wherever they bloody well please, warriors wasting their guts on oncoming traffic. The English are absolutely terrific at war. The Falklands Conflict, which nearly lost me a group of otherwise intelligent and worldly local friends when I referred to it as a 'skirmish', was the most unbuttoned period I can recall on the streets of London. Nostalgic courage was in the air, strangers compared notes on street corners, women looked brighter and the men looked a little taller.

I like Oxford Street particularly from the back of a taxi or the top of a bus. Above the hotchpotch of shop-fronts that turn it into an open bazaar at ground level, superstructures heavy on cherubs and cornucopiae show off the solid – the infrangible – pretensions of tradesmen who established business there in the nineteenth century, many still trading, others defunct.

'Remember Marshall and Snelgrove?' I asked the driver.

'Big store, wannit?' he said. 'Before my time, really.'

Marshall and Snelgrove went down in the 1970s, so my driver was not much more than 25 in spite of the balding patch about the size of a ten-penny piece on his crown. It's odd how London working men do nothing to hide their tendency to premature baldness; in fact they like to crop their hair short and wear the bald patch as a badge of honour, marking the gulf between themselves and the upper-class English whose silky hair flops into their eyes. Whatever yearning used to exist among young Londoners to ape their so-called betters once upon a time has gone into reverse and has tipped in the easier direction: the day after my son left his prep school he and his fellows shaved their heads, fitted earrings, and dropped all aspirates from their speech.

'If I ever keep pets again,' I heard myself start, in spite of knowing how much I was going to regret it, 'it will be a couple of cats called "Marshall and Snelgrove". Good names for London toms, don't you think?'

Ageing entails regularly making a fool of oneself in the eyes of youngsters, who have started to draw back and give me the fish-eye when I indulge in whimsical babble. 'Mind you, I've always wanted a Persian cat so I could call it "Eternity".'

I'd gone too far too fast; I couldn't stop.

'Then when friends rang and asked me what I was up to, I could tell them, "I'm brushing 'Eternity' . . .".'

Apparently my driver chose to blame the flaky stream-of-consciousness coming from his back-seat on national character rather than senile dementia, for after a pause he asked: 'Been here long, then?'

'Thirty years.'

I turned my head away so he could not see in the mirror when I mouthed his reply with him: 'Guess-you-must-like-it-here.'

Right on cue, a micro-beat after I'd anticipated it, he delivered the next line: 'Haven't-lost-your-accent-though.'

'Reckon not, pahdner,' I drawled in bad fake-Texan.

That got a chuckle. As usual.

'So-what-part-of-the-States-you-from-then?'

'New York,' I replied, and I sent up a prayer that he be not one of them who had been there: 'O, let him, please, be one of the others!'

At that moment, en route to the dentist, in spite of having started the habitual ball rolling, the last thing I wanted was an engagement of any emotional depth. And the trouble is I cannot hear my old home-town maligned or even just misunderstood without rising to a spirited defence. On the other hand when a stranger likes New York, his enthusiasm for it drives me into sentimental reminiscence. 'Me and the wife went to Florida last year,' he said.

'Hallelujah!' cried the inner voice. 'He be one of the others!'

'Go to Disney World?' I asked, trying to sound as if I didn't know.

Sometimes I long for the old days when America used to be as strange and distant as the moon to Londoners. My nationality gave me an exotic cachet back then. Now there's hardly a barrow boy or London cabbie who hasn't been over the pond, some to Manhattan, a few with specialised interests have made it to San Francisco, Vegas or New Orleans, and at a guess every last one of the remaining hundreds of thousands has been to Disney World in Florida.

'My wife thought I was crazy, said it was for kids. I told her I didn't want to wait that long, until we had kids. It was wicked. All them great rides and stuff. I want to go back, maybe see New York next time.'

'No kids yet?'

'One on the way,' he said and fell into a reverie.

In peace for a moment, I admired his light grip on the wheel in the classic ten-to-two position. Twelve years earlier, already no spring chicken, I thought I wanted to leave London, to live deep in the country far from public transport, and with that plan in mind I finally had to learn to drive. Keith my instructor was lean, stretched, damaged and brave: a driven man. He had served on a submarine during the war and when he saw my perfectly logical tight-lipped terror of every other driver on the road, it reminded him of how scared he used to be when his sub was under attack: scared shitless, he didn't mind saying.

'Our loos flush up you know, back on to the surface of the ocean. And believe me, they could have marked where we passed by what was floating there.'

Often when I'm snug behind a London cabbie, I compare the sly London style of driving with California vanity driving or Parisian impatience or New York gridlock, and fondly I remember Keith.

'Drive su-ee-cidally!' he used to command on the flat, clenching his long, knobbed fingers into fists on the dashboard.

Eventually I passed the test, whereupon I moved immediately, not to the country, but perversely right into the very muscle of London where I live now, and I haven't been behind the wheel of a car since.

My driver swung off Oxford Street to avoid traffic jams caused by road repairs ahead. London's central streets are in a constant state of primordial upheaval. Suddenly our fickle island sky darkened and a few drops of rain hit the windscreen.

'Starting to spit,' I said.

'They said on the radio . . .'

'Got it right for once . . . cold . . .'

'My wife . . . central heating . . . yesterday. We was that cold.'

'Remember . . . summer . . . 76?'

He couldn't have been more than a kid in 76, but it had been a legendary heat-wave and he whistled softly through his front teeth.

'Hot,' we said in unison.

'Weather's changing,' he said.

'One thing never changes: holiday weekend you can bet . . .' I began, and together we said: '. . . piss down rain.'

A taxi going the other way aligned with ours at a red light. The lone passenger, a ginger-haired man in a dark suit, was leaning his chin on his hand and staring out of the window. I wondered if he was having a version of the weather-conversation with his driver too, and if it accounted for his long face. But the window between them was firmly closed. Probably he was in the enviable state of transcendental contemplation a London cab is designed to induce except of course in compulsive American chatterboxes like me. Then again I thought, as our taxis pulled out on their opposite ways, England is a nation of tea-drinkers and tea is notoriously binding; chances were that the ginger-haired man, like so many Londoners unfairly accused of being distant and standoffish, was in fact reflecting disconsolately on the state of his lower bowel. The gut is destiny too in its way.

Our approach to Mr Rabin's practice crossed a section of the Edgware Road where there is always heavy motor traffic yet at the same time so little bustle on the pavements it seems to be in a different time-zone from Marble Arch, just 100 yards away. Shopkeepers leaned on their door-frames gazing out, behind them heaps of designer luggage, and babies' clothes, and ornate gilded furniture. Heavy curtains covered the windows of the coffee-shops and restaurants; at the newsagents only a few men browsed the racks of papers in Arabic type. Not many women were to be seen; those out and about were shrouded in black. One could sense that under their robes they were sullen and quick to anger. When I was a little girl, there were still streets in New York City that could have been transported whole to the lower East Side from Warsaw, Vilna, Minsk, where shopkeepers sold dill pickles out of barrels on the sidewalks and spoke volubly to my father in Yiddish while stroking my hair with wrinkled hands that trailed the smell of vinegar. London tends to scatter and absorb immigrants and iron them swiftly into the general fabric. When an ethnic group claims a few blocks for itself – Bengalis in Spitalfields, West Indians in Brixton, Chinatown in the West End, rich Arabs in Bayswater and Regent's Park – the atmosphere seems downbeat and drab to someone who has known the vivid colonies that made up New York's mosaic, and continue to this day. Immigrants to the New World came in hope, a few still do. But London has had to contain factions squeezed out of a collapsing empire, and a lot of them arrive defensive and sulky like grown children who are forced by circumstances to live with mother.

Two men in long robes and chequered head-dresses stepped out in front of us on to a zebra crossing. They were frowning and one of them was running worry-beads through his fingers.

'Tea towels,' said my driver, sounding amiable.

There was no oncoming traffic so we crossed diagonally so he could drop me right in front of my destination. Mr Rabin's surgery is on the ground floor of one of several big ugly blocks of red brick on the edge of genteel leafy Bayswater. Only five or six of the original Georgian buildings have survived speculators' greed or German bombs, whichever it was – probably both – that ruined Kendal Street's integrity. They are all now cheap hotels and the street is forgettable in the landscape except, of course, to those of us with a reason to remember it. Passengers usually choose to pay their drivers from inside the cab, but whatever the weather I prefer to pay from the pavement giving us both a chance to size each other up face to face. After all, he and I have generally been sharing a conversation of some intensity, he with an image in his mirror, I with the back of a head. When he reached for the five-pound note and looked at me I felt the usual momentary surprise to find myself at home in a blue-eyed city. He, I could see, had the feeling he should know me from somewhere, shouldn't he? There exists a special variety of urban *idiot savant* whose gift is to be able to spot from a distance and call by name anyone who has flickered, no matter how briefly across a TV screen, be it in an ad, on the news, on a panel, or as a corpse in a hospital drama. It is a phenomenal little quirk which, sad to say, is accompanied by morbid excitement and confusion in all other areas. Among normal people the TV recognition factor for talking heads lasts about three days after each appearance. Over the years I have appeared on TV often enough, however, to have accumulated a shadowy after-image in the memories of many perfectly well-adjusted Londoners. As I usually pontificate on 'women's issues', I could rest assured there wasn't much danger a man like my cabbie was going to pass the point of thinking he knew me, he knew he knew me, I was confident he wouldn't quite place where he knew me from.

As for him, I knew him pretty well. He liked his pint down the pub with the lads; he'd recently cut down on fags and was putting on weight; out from behind the wheel he'd move with a pugilistic bounce passed down through generations of ye olde chirpy cockneys. No small icons dangled from his dashboard, but soon a small framed snapshot of his firstborn would be tucked into the sun-shield. He hadn't been to church since his wedding; nevertheless, if you asked him – I often did – he'd say: 'It didn't come out of nuffink, did it? It was sunfink, for sure.' His left ear was pierced, but he no longer wore the earring, hadn't for years. In bed he was husky and stubby. He would be faithful to his wife except by accident, accidents will happen, and faithful to West Ham football team until he died. More racist than his father or grandfather, less sexist: live and let live was his motto. As soon as he and his wife had children they were going to move out of the flat in east London to deepest Essex where they could raise them within sight of trees and open spaces.

The cab was pulling away when out of one in the row of small hotels across the street emerged two women wrapped to the ground in black robes and yashmaks. They scurried footlessly in the light rain towards a grey Mercedes at the curb where a man in traditional dress waiting for them looked carefully over their heads into the middle distance. As the door of the hotel was closing slowly behind the women I saw a cage with a large bird in it standing behind an oak reception desk. And on the instant, a light switched on in a dark corner of my mind: 30 years ago, my first home in London was a bed-sitter in Kendal Street, near Marble Arch, directly across from where I stood and from the man who, unknown to me then, was later to become my dentist. Of course I hadn't forgotten my rented room in Kendal Street. It is bound to cross my mind, at the very least whenever I have my teeth checked, and I will be able to describe it in some detail long after I have forgotten more recent places. But the texture and heat of the memory had faded into the past, all that remained was as terse as an extract from the obituary of someone who once a long time ago called herself by my name: 'Arriving in London in 1963, she made her first London home in Kendal Street . . .' Then the two alien women slid into the back-seat of their car, I caught a glimpse behind them of the interior of number 51 Kendal Street, unchanged after more than thirty years, and memory beyond words rushed home with a reek of boiled cabbage and the squawk of a caged bird.

2

Victoria Station

A few months ago a letter arrived on my desk from a man whose name meant absolutely nothing to me. He told me he'd seen my byline in a newspaper and he wondered if I was the same Irma Kurtz with whom three decades earlier he had shared a compartment on the train from Paris to London.

'I was a law student at the time. You'd been living in Paris. You were emigrating to England. You told me you were determined to be a writer.'

The business about being a writer had to be an extrapolation of hindsight; never in a million years would I have had the nerve to make any such claim.

I rang the number on his letterhead, he worked in the administrative department of a chain of supermarkets, and we arranged to meet for tea the following week at the Groucho Club in central London where I've been a member since the club opened in the 1980s. My flat is nearby and I arrived early and sat at a small table near the door so the burden of recognition would fall on him. I had forgotten him altogether; what made me so sure he'd know me? When he and I had last met I'd been in my twenties, unwrinkled and without spectacles, my hair waist-length and still wholly chestnut brown. It was late afternoon, the literary let's-do-lunch-ers had all gone back to work, the slick cruisers of the music business had not yet mounted their nightly assault on Groucho's bar, and in the event my man recognised me immediately because nobody else was there except me and my old friend Jeffrey Bernard dozing in his wheelchair.

During the next hour he and I talked politely about our jobs and careers. He told me about his wife and grown-up children. When we met on the train he had been training to be a barrister and he'd ended up in the supermarket business: disappointment was implicit I would have said, though none showed on his comfortable face. As for me, determined as he remembered I was to write with a capital 'W', I'm known in London mostly for dishing out advice to the lovelorn in a glossy magazine.

'A dirty job,' I said, 'but someone has to do it.'

It did not happen with us as it does with Barnard graduates of my year when they pass through London and look me up, that after the initial shock time's tread-marks start to vanish so in a little while we find ourselves young again in each other's eyes, and the world seems younger too. He remained a roundish, greyish businessman on the edge of retirement, a householder who paid his bills on time, a grown-up *and* a likely Volvo driver. Once, looking up from my vodka and tonic, for I'd decided to have a real drink instead of tea, I surprised a glint of folly in his eyes, but when we shook hands on the pavement outside the Groucho and wished each other luck, we knew we were never going to meet again. A taxi was pulling in to him like a bull to a matador and I had already turned to walk home, when suddenly I realised that due to a very English kind of restraint, I was about to let a golden opportunity go by.

'Wait!' I called out to him. 'What was I like?'

'You?' he said, pausing as he entered the cab. 'Why, I'd never met a girl as brave as you.'

He had the wrong Irma Kurtz, for sure. Or one of us was crazy. Thirty years and more ago when I arrived in London I was scared and desperate. It must have been the coat I was wearing that had him fooled. It was black broadcloth, French, fitted to the hips then slightly flared: a very classy coat, very sure of itself – it was also the single garment I have ever had money and nerve enough to buy in Paris. It cost exactly half the 100 dollars that stood between me and destitution. This was back in the early 1960s remember, when nice girls still wore white gloves in the evening and, especially in Paris, there was hardly any manoeuvring space between being a lady and being a slob. The Parisian shop-girl who sold me the coat was a few years my senior. Her earrings were the right design in a base metal, her hair was a tint or two out of fashion, and her scarf, though it had been perfectly settled into the neck of her fashionable shift dress, was not quite Hermes: she was all in all designed to be a bare degree or two less well turned out than her clientele. She snatched the money from my hand and hurried me out before my shaggy silhouette and air of suicidal bravado gave the place a bad name. But I had my brave new coat and a carrier-bag too, imprinted 'Rue du Faubourg Saint-Honoré', in which to pack a couple of towels and some underwear for the exodus to England. Later, I toted the bag around London until it disintegrated one damp morning outside Marble Arch Underground station.

For me, unhappiness resides in Paris. There are neighbourhoods – the Place de la Contrescarpe, for example, a short stretch on the Boulevard Arago, the top end of the long, long rue de Vaugirard, the Palais de Justice, the Île Saint-Louis – where I trailed so much dumb anguish in my youth that the stones throw it back to me when I pass that way now, and the prowling wet-cat smell of the Seine at night stings my eyes again the way heartbreak used to do. Standing at the window of our room – suddenly all mine – on the Île Saint-Louis, I watched Douglas fold his long self into the back-seat of my then best friend's car for a lift south, and I knew that whatever we'd told each other, that was the end of us. Paris saw the end of my first great love affair, true enough. But it was Paris herself who let me down, the pestilential tart. Mine was a terrible earnest generation of Americans and I never dreamed when Paris broke my heart that I would ever again be able to fall as hard for any other city.

I did not simply want to live in Paris: when I started out from America, I wanted to be Parisian. In my mind to be Parisian meant coming as close as anyone could to perfection of intellect and art and experience and style and sex. My notion of being Parisian was nearly as absurdly glorious as the Parisians' own. Back in the 1950s, when I was about the age my son is now, we young people were neither proud nor rebellious in any clearly defined way, and we had no pretensions to a 'youth culture'. Europe, especially Paris, was the wildest of all romances for questing Americans of my generation, and Art with a capital 'A' represented to us all that could truly be free: free spirit, free time, free speech, free love. Boatloads of us sailed abroad every summer to seek out Art and Paris. Paris and Art were the kind of threat to educated young Americans of the post-war era that drugs and pushers are now. After a few months of flirting with existential possibilities and making some tentative love with poetical French waiters or scrounging expatriate American writers, nine-tenths of my coevals returned safely to roost, the cosmopolitan gloss on their feathers fading quickly under the indirect lighting of home. But others became art-junkies who eventually accumulated in the least demanding Mediterranean countries where colonies of them still survive, cracked expatriates, dry as old leather, parched of every appetite except for grappa or ouzo or Fundador, and gossip.

As for me, early on I had contracted wanderlust, a relatively rare condition among females of the nesting age, and one way or another we women are born to nest for most of our lives. Not more than a day or two after I'd learned my name, the very first feeling I recall was yearning for the hoot of an ocean liner putting out to sea in the Hudson Bay within earshot of my bedroom window; the tug of that sound on my soul and the need to follow it was as omnipotent as hunger. Wanderlust: it defies explanation or cure. It is a crazy homesickness that drives the afflicted away from home, it is a pathological curiosity that in my case pre-dated imagination and subsumed it. From the moment a curious woman sets out to see the world, she postpones until God knows when the domestic need to create or procreate a world of her own. Wander-lust has turned me into a sort of journeyman anthropologist, not unlike Margaret Mead, another Barnard graduate it so happens, though in spite of what has been said about her, I cannot seriously believe she fornicated with her natives.

When I arrived in Paris, two years after university and determined to live there, I had not one friend in the city, least of all friendly work-mates at my job. Teaching English at Berlitz was dull, dead-end work, no matter how often a girl told herself James Joyce had done it too in his day, and perhaps sat at her very desk trying to make his own ambitious shop-keepers absorb the difference between 'looking at' and 'looking into'. The other teachers were male to a man and all from England; ageing remittance men who were less able every day to return to a homeland which though geographically around the corner had already receded a million miles from the way they remembered it. They were a broken-down old crew it seemed to me who resented the new Parisian infatuation with Hollywood, and were piqued that I had been hired for pupils requesting lessons in 'American' instead of 'English'. My accent and idiom threatened their last reason for pride, their language; that was my explanation for why they were so nasty to me. They were my first Englishmen en masse. I wasn't the seasoned Anglo-hand I was fated to become, not by a long shot, and I hadn't a clue what made them tick. How could I know that their mocking badinage – 'Tell me, dear girl, can you actually teach them to enunciate while they're chewing gum?' – wasn't intended to offend? On the contrary, the nudging mock is an Englishman's way of being friendly.

A few days before every pay-day there I'd be again, living on soup and yoghurts, returning the glass pots for the deposits. Tourists didn't know that Metro tickets were valid for a round-trip in those days, and a knowledgeable girl could travel free on one-punch tickets she picked up off the pavements near American Express. I wasn't flat broke, I'd waitressed for a year and a half in New York to put aside a nest-egg, but it was earmarked for travel one sunny day in Italy and Spain, and certainly not to be wasted on mere subsistence. The flea-pit where I lived was called 'Le Grand Hôtel de France', sardonically only by accident; Parisians are never sardonic. A classic left-bank mix of students and prostitutes who lived there could have been the cast of an operetta except they were all unmusical, unfriendly and glum. The hotel bath was grimy and hot water was in short supply, so once a week I used to go to the public baths off the Boulevard Saint-Michel where there were big stall showers in which an American girl could wash her hair. The attendant set a timer beside each cubicle, then pounded on the door to let customers know when their allotted twenty minutes was up. A chorus of song in Arabic and gutter French rose with the steam. I didn't mind the squalor. Who of my art-sick generation would have minded it? Just as during my solitary walks when the city glowed and sparkled, always just ahead like lights seen from a rudderless ship, all I had to do was whisper: 'Paris, I'm in Paris . . .' to ease for a moment the melancholy and the persistent weary longing that together made a feeling curiously like boredom. Loneliness, longing, discomfort and ennui too, at the time – I considered them part of the price I had to pay for independence. Looking back, I see that I was quite correct.

One Saturday in March I was on my way back to 'Le Grand Etcetera' from the public baths. It was cool and my hair was still wet, so I thought I'd take myself somewhere warm for a coffee. In the bag over my shoulder was a copy of *L'Étranger*. I was working through it in French, and it was something to hide behind while I sat alone among the chattering students from the Sorbonne who packed the local cafés, as was their right. Suddenly, coming towards me out of the crowd on the pavement, was someone I knew. Someone I really knew! A girl from my year at Barnard.

'Rhoda! Rhoda Edwards!'

Anyone seeing us hug and leap around the left-bank boulevard would have taken us for refugee sisters; there was even a slight physical resemblance, though it was more a matter of style: we were both still turned out in the uniform of the arty set at our college: tight jeans and baggy sweatshirts – to show how little we cared for appearances, how we cared even less for men who cared for appearances, see? And if the bemused and critical double-takes I'd begun to expect from passing Parisians were anything to go by, it worked.

Rho and I had known each other as undergraduates but we more or less lost touch at the start of our third year when she switched suddenly from reading English Literature to Political Science, whatever that was. One noisy afternoon she'd berated me in the lunch-room because she overheard me tell a Freshman that the very mention of Virginia Woolf made me want to rush out and sleep with Russian sailors – a piece of virginal swank, by the by, for I had not yet slept with anybody. Fraternity parties made me sick and Donald, the man on whom I had a great crush, was gay – in those days he called himself 'queer'. Virgins in their late teens and early twenties were thick on the ground way back then, before the pill, when sex education was a course set by Fred and Ginger. At our college Contract Bridge was a bigger threat to scholarship than sex, and we swats wouldn't play either game. Rhoda, on the other hand, had an honest-to-God lover. He was called Henry, or more often Hank. Hank was a postgraduate at Princeton, and at weekends he and Rhoda lived together, absolutely everyone in our year knew, in a genuine love-nest somewhere uptown. Gosh. When we bumped into each other, she told me right away that she was there with Hank, *because* of Hank, who even as we spoke was at work on the great American novel, an undertaking which in those days required its author to live in Paris.

During the years ahead when Hank and Rhoda and I were going to live and travel together in Greece, Yugoslavia, Turkey and Spain, she never tanned; an illness in adolescence had left her skin deeply pockmarked and it held a chill even in Mediterranean summer. Nevertheless she was quite vain, especially of her long thick hair; it was a beautiful reddish brown, exactly the same colour as her eyes and of late sunsets, so when the sun happened to set behind Rho it absorbed her hair and eyes, and left a rough, white mask floating against the auburn sky. Except when she was flirting, a wary, weary expression and the downturn of her mouth made her look much older than I, though we were the same age within weeks. We laughed a lot in those days, even Rhoda, though she always laughed grudgingly. I never saw her cry. The set of Rhoda's opinions was the oldest thing about her: snappish, cranky and inflexible. Art, movies, books, food, the weather, and especially on human behaviour, her pronouncements were decisive and beyond debate. Rhoda *was* her opinions; to challenge the least of them had to be a personal attack. To mistake self-importance for self-confidence was a common miscalculation of my youth. It seemed to me at the time that she was the last word in assured intellectual prowess. Besides, I was not thinking at all clearly, hardly thinking at all, when we met in Paris. How long had it been since I'd found myself one of a couple of friends, talking in a café over a drink?

'Shlepping is in our blood,' I said, referring to the big bag much like my own that was over her shoulder.

'We're a couple of New Yorkers, that's for sure,' she said.

Gratitude for our similarities and for company in that Gaulish desert welled up in me, indistinguishable from love.

Hank was trim and muscular in a rather dainty fashion. Big ears, bushy eyebrows and wire-rimmed glasses looked of a piece – I wondered if before he went to sleep he laid them as one strange object on the bedside-table, then put them all on again together in the morning. He had Groucho Marx's lope down to perfection, with a cigarette instead of a cigar between his teeth which were already edged in brown from the perpetual Gauloise stuck to his lower lip. He did other imitations too, including one of an inexperienced hen on her nest that made me laugh until it hurt. In his early teens he'd been an actor on Broadway. Not only had he kept good timing and a professionally slick delivery, he could bluff his way out of traffic tickets, late payment of bills, the nosiness of border guards, and a weak pair against aces. But he tried not to clown around too much, Rhoda didn't like it, and anyhow, philosophical debate with lavish literary references was the approved gambit of the left-bank café scene. Hank's rhetorical style was masculine and hectoring; once in a while I'd come up with an observation to stop him in mid-flow, and he'd look at me, head cocked, wondering where in hell I'd read that? As he grew older he looked increasingly mild, except for his eyes, and ever more like the brains behind a bloody old revolution. All in all, Hank was the archetypal clever Jew, I guess, with lots of body hair who appeals particularly to bookish Christian women.

Hank and Rhoda were both accomplished liars, particularly by omission. Even after we'd travelled together for more than a year they could side-step my direct questions skilfully when one of their secrets was in danger.

'Truth,' Hank said, in grand mode, 'should not be fucked up with facts, and an artist deals only in truth.'

Rhoda, who favoured the knowing smile that allows flattering assumptions, managed to look as if she'd thought of it first and let Hank say it for her. Complicity and the exchange of glances gave their sojourn in Europe the drama of a flight from danger that made my own little odyssey feel really quite timid. Also, Hank had money so they could devote themselves to Art and to talking.

From the moment I met Rhoda and went back with her to the room in the hotel very like my own where she and Hank were staying, my life in Paris became more convivial. After work, instead of reading Colette over a cold dinner out of tins and waxed paper in my room, I hurried to meet my friends along with the gang at the Café Tournon, a few streets away in the Latin Quarter. In my memory, the Tournon bulges like a cartoon saloon in Loony Toonville, and pulsates with noise and smoke pouring out of disaffected American blacks and young men still milking the GI Bill who drank there every night. Parisians who gate-crashed the Tournon were feverish for American cars, movies, cigarettes, for all things American in fact, except intense long-haired girls from New York in jeans and sweatshirts. Behind the cash register reigned la patronne, busy and bad-tempered, wearing a stiff black wig à la Cleopatra. The old timers said her hair never grew back after it was shaved off in punishment for collaboration during the war. Day after day she watched us with disgust and hostility so silent and ancient I can't believe she was any sweeter to the Nazis than she was to us, cadging drinks from each other under her evil eye, and talking, talking, talking the nights away. Words, words, words, mostly in English, in French too, they swirl around my memory of Paris. What has become of all those words? Coins spent in the streaming past, I cannot touch them now.

Not long after we met, Hank bought a one-bedroom flat on the Boulevard Arago that was soon an alternative hang-out for habitués of the Tournon. Chestnut trees swept the big windows. When in leaf they muted the irritable, high-pitched noise of Parisian traffic three flights below. Directly across the street was the Sante Prison. Sometimes at night prisoners suddenly began to howl and strum their metal cups across the bars of their cages, and whenever they did Hank interrupted the talking and called for a moment's silence while he stood by the window with his eyes closed, swaying back and forth to the dismal racket filtering through the branches in to us, as if it were a call to prayer. Perhaps it was. Hank had run into William Burroughs a couple of times at La Coupole. Devoted as he was to the older man's work, even more he hungered for the rackety life that inspired it. Like Burroughs, Hank through no fault of his own had inherited a small fortune, but he was not so adroit as Burroughs at hiding it. Word that he was loaded was out in the quarter, known scroungers were perpetually sidling up to him in the cafés, and if Rhoda hadn't stuck as close as glue, there is no question he would have given all his money away. Hank's trouble was that as much as he wanted to be rid of his filthy lucre so he could settle down in the gutter and write a masterpiece, he was at the same time fiercely competitive, and about the only thing he'd learned from his military service in America was how to play poker. When Hank was playing poker, which he did to a professional standard, not words, not jokes, not even Art mattered more than winning. No, let me be precise: once the hand was dealt, nothing on earth was more important to Hank than beating every other guy at the table.

Years down our devious, unmapped road, Hank was going to buy a magnificent old yacht called *Stormsvalla*. My then lover, Douglas and I helped him and Rhoda and some others deliver her from the Isle of Wight to the Mediterranean where Hank planned to charter her to tourists out of Cannes. Douglas and I stayed on as crew. During the long weeks in port while we waited for paying customers fool enough to put out to sea with a bunch of amateurs in a twelve-metre racing yacht, Hank's skill at the table was our main support. It was enough to spread the word in a few dockside cafés about a game on board, and punters arrived in relays especially after the American fleet sailed in. Whenever sessions looked like lasting through the night, Rhoda used to stay ashore in an hotel and leave me to look after the players; there wasn't much I could do to kill time between calls for drinks and sandwiches but walk on deck above the main saloon and look down at the men through the skylights. From secretly observing men play poker, seeing how they bet, how they tricked the other guys and most of all how they tricked themselves, I learned more about their fears and bravado, their cowboy fantasies, their impulsive and romantic nature, than ever any woman learned in bed. One dawn I was watching a day-old game that had already claimed a number of victims. A Texan, slightly older than the run of players, was holding his own and had coolly side-stepped every ambush Hank laid for him. They broke for a few minutes so the Texan could go for a pee, and Hank came up on deck to snort at a proprietary inhaler that was widely believed to contain an amphetamine. He saw me and walked over to where I was standing by the skylight that looked down on the table.

'Met your match, Hank? Tex is nearly as sneaky as you are.'

'You know, Kurtz,' he said, 'you and I together, we could work out a way to cheat. With you up here seeing every hand, it wouldn't be hard to do.'

I turned away; I was scared. He shrugged, laughed, and went below deck to play. Topside, counting stars and shore-lights, I'd had enough of watching men play poker. Although Hank and I remained friends for a long time to come, on that point our destinies parted crucially. Nowaday, I cannot picture Hank as a man heading for 70, it is much easier to assume that he is dead.

Instantaneously, from the very first day we met in Paris, we three became a tiny state of America. In the summer, when I was sacked after the boss overheard me reading to an advanced class from William Faulkner instead of the Berlitz phrase book, we rented a Moorish watch-tower on the Mallorcan coast for a few months. 'Big Irma', Hank started calling me then, not because of my size, which was on the skinny side; because I did not mind gutting fish, or cleaning out the primitive loo when it was blocked. Sex was about the only thing we did not do together, although there was one sultry afternoon in Spain when Rhoda floated an erotic invitation to a threesome. I was too romantic and innocent to take her up on it. Besides, I did not fancy either of them physically. When we left the island in September, we hitch-hiked from Barcelona to Istanbul. Why not? There were no motorways then, roads occurred where they were needed, and while we meandered across countries and over frontiers, I felt my first remembered wish nearly coming true: to track the planet inch by inch, under countless new skies. Back in Paris at last, when our adventures on the road had ended, Hank returned to his novel. Rhoda told me he had given himself, or she had given him, two more years abroad to finish and publish it. Rhoda later would go on and on about the child who lives inside each of us, and how unhappy was the one who lived in her. But as the Parisian winter began to bite it was the discontented adult within myself who started to grumble and goad me: 'Get up, you lazy girl. This isn't the life for you. You're not getting any younger you know. Listen to me, silly child, do you want to end up brain-dead in a Parisian language school? Go home. Go back where real life is. Get a real job.'

Finally, I could take no more of my smug, nagging inner voice and I spent what was left of my nest-egg on a cheap passage to New York.

Before the lights of Europe had dipped under the horizon, I knew I was making a mistake. My imagination lacked a space in it for America. Even when New York was roaring around me again, I couldn't imagine myself there: it was the reverse of my relationship with Paris where I imagined myself all the time, but could not be. And London: London? London never entered my mind.

In Manhattan a job came up in fashion publicity where my evident disregard for the business gave me a funny kind of authority among the flibberty-gibbets. I wrote captions and press releases and sent them out to newspapers all over America, then when the clippings came in I pasted them into a scrapbook for our clients while taking private delight in how many fashion editors used my words verbatim under their own bylines. Meanwhile, a stream of letters flowed out to Hank and Rhoda full of jokes about the job, and impatience, and dreams of returning to Paris. Now I can see that it was then, in the humiliating aftermath of a first failed attempt, that the seal was stamped upon my eventual expatriation. When at last I'd saved enough to go abroad and try again, it was going to have to be do or die. Not only was my pride at stake; time was starting to turn against me: I was still young, yes, but never would I be young enough again to pick up a destiny in America. On the next try I'd have to make a life of some quality abroad, or to hell with it: I'd stay there anyway and become another dull expat, like many I'd seen, stranded overseas and clinging to the husks of what had once been grand passions: some for gambling, others for drink, some for their own sex, and many like me, for Paris herself, false and seductive.

A Parisian couturière on holiday in New York paid part of my fare for bringing her fourteen suitcases with me on the boat; she was crossing by plane which was still a dashing, expensive way to travel at the start of the 1960s. From behind bulwarks of luggage in the taxi I looked out again at my city-love. Unlike most loves revisited it was frozen in recollected beauty, and unchanged in a way that ought to have made me suspicious, I now see. But it took my breath. I could hardly have spoken for happiness. Merrily, I danced into the old bohemian domesticity, staying by choice at 'Le Grand Whatsit', and diving straight back into the turbulent scene at the Tournon where the talking, talking, talking closed over my head like a quilted comforter.

The Paris couturier and the most elegant man on earth, Hubert de Givenchy, employed me out of courtesy to Ruth Hammer, my former boss in New York, and one of his good friends. Neither he nor I knew what I was supposed to do for him, except please to keep myself out of sight of the clients, though I was allowed to watch them surreptitiously from behind a Gobelin arras, no less. I saw Hank and Rhoda of course, though not as much as I had in the old days. Hank had taken to sleeping all day and writing through the night when he felt a stronger creative urge, and thanks to temperament as well as necessity my time-keeping has always been the contrary. Rhoda had started writing poetry while I was in America; she wasn't ready to let anyone read it, but she let me believe it must be pretty good. Then just before my two-week summer holiday, I met a young German woman at La Coupole who was driving down to a Spanish island called Ibiza that was practically unknown in those days. She offered me a lift with her in exchange for expenses. Why not?

A tall blue-eyed man from Argentina helped me on to the island off the weekly boat from Barcelona. His name was Douglas Sibbald – the proto-hippies of the small foreign community called him 'The Silver Fox' because of his prematurely white hair which was luxurious and gorgeous, and not practical for everyday wear. He was by profession both a sailor and a goldsmith. Three days after we met we were alone in a dinghy, neither of us wearing much, only the sparkling sea, the sky, and one another to look at, when suddenly I heard quite distinctly from out of nowhere, out of everywhere, the sound of breaking glass – hey presto! Just like that, I had fallen in love for the first time. Sometimes I wonder if life isn't a form struggling to achieve symmetry any little way it can out of a mess. Oddly enough two decades later another tall man was going to help me on to another island; he too was blue-eyed and had silver hair. There was no sound on that occasion. He and Douglas are the handsome bookends either side of the shelf of paperbacks that compose my love-life.

It was to be more than a year before I returned to Paris with Douglas. A friend of a friend helped me to a job writing feature articles for the *US Army Times* in its office on the rue Cambon. Meanwhile, Rhoda had put away her poems and was painting abstracts in oil. The Great American Novel, long past its allotted gestation, remained a ragged typescript that had been toted from hotel rooms all over Europe to rented Moorish towers in Spain, to a captain's chest on board *Stormsvalla*, and always back to Paris.

'He promised me he was an Artist,' Rhoda said in a moment of uncharacteristic candour. 'But he's only a playboy.'

'Don't be silly, Rho,' I said, 'who ever heard of a playboy with dandruff.'

Trouble between them could not be taken seriously. Their familiar battery of conspiratorial exchanges in code and glances continued, even though I had to admit a lot of the signals I intercepted were starting to be charged with anger, and on Hank's part, with apology.

My new job was to supply the *US Army Times* with weekly pieces about the Louvre, the guillotine, the Metro, the sewers and any other Parisian thing that would not inflame over-sexed American soldiers on leave. Hank called me 'the saltpetre of journalism . . .'. When Douglas wasn't delivering yachts he stayed with me in a room I had saved and scrounged money to buy on the Île Saint-Louis. It was just the end of a corridor, no wider than a railway carriage, and we had to share an atmospheric Turkish-style toilet on the landing with other tenants. But a fourteenth-century beam spanned the ceiling and our window looked out on a street practically unchanged for five centuries. Gradually it began to dawn on me that what Douglas had to say for himself, so captivating in Mediterranean sunshine and so sexy late at night on *Stormsvalla*'s deck while dolphins cut streaks of phosphorus in the ocean around us, had begun to sound awfully fey in Paris where hard-nosed existentialism still festered. He wasn't a city-boy. The big rootless romance of a sea-going man, which I understood only too well, found itself in him up against the jeweller's need to miniaturise and contain. He was of the New Age, 30 years ahead of his time. Whenever he softly and insistently interrupted the ceaseless talk to describe the enchantments of whales' songs, say, or the healing powers of turquoise, I'd cringe to see the look that passed between Hank and Rho. More and more I found myself torn between shame for my lover and a fierce, tender desire to protect him.

Then one ugly night we had trouble with the law, and when Hank and Rhoda decided soon afterwards to go back to Spain Douglas jumped at the chance for a lift. He could barely hide his eagerness to leave Paris, and me. One week after he'd gone, a woman we'd known in the neighbourhood returned from a holiday on Ibiza. She bumped into me at a local café and told me right away that she had seen Douglas, and that he was living with a blonde model from California. I don't think she meant any harm. How could she know I had not yet learned how to fall out of love? But what was as bad as the end of my first great love, in fact it was much worse, was that Paris and I were breaking up too.

Cities are only human. And Paris is a stunning transvestite, overbearing and narrow-minded, all false charm and made for novelty – there is nothing she prefers to her own image. Policemen armed with sub-machine guns defend her reflection in the glass, so it never shows less than gorgeous. I came upon them once near the Place de la Contrescarpe while they were beating the teeth out of a young Algerian. Gunfire was often heard in the streets back then, and not a word about it in the papers next day.

But the sound most typical of Paris was the clanging shut every night of the metal grilles over doors and windows. The sudden revelation that my future in Paris was doomed to every kind of failure set me into a tailspin. (*European capital deranged by grief* (7): despair.) I drank too much for the first time in my life, not the last, and I slept around – of all ways to dissipate grief, sleeping around is the loneliest.

Then one wintry night an English newspaper reporter who used to drink with me gave me a complimentary ticket to a touring performance of *King Lear* with Paul Scofield in the role. Afterwards, alone on the walk back from the Place de l'Opéra to my room, I stopped to hang over the rail of the Pont Marie and put my frosty breath up against the night. In that setting made for disappointed romantics to ponder theatrically whether to end their lives, I was thinking how I could save mine, and where. Paris would be the death of me if I stayed, I'd trail along behind her, cast off and unwelcome, subsisting on cheap meals and shameful memories. As for America, the only city I knew or took seriously was New York, and I had emphatically forsworn New York from the deck of my last boat as it was putting out to sea; the disgrace of going back would be ruinous. Besides, America was too far from all my curiosity. It was then, while the oily black water of the Seine flowed under me and some of the greatest words in English still sang in my brain, that London for the first time presented itself as an option. 'Weary and grey', I'd written in my journal the first time I'd been there during a summer break from Columbia. But I had visited several times since then and the city had started to exert a stealthy charm on me, like a quiet man who keeps turning up in crowded rooms until a woman hardly knows how it has happened she has begun to expect him and look for him. And, oh my, when he speaks at last, what a beautiful language he uses.

And that is how a little while later, had anyone been watching, I could have been seen in my brave black coat getting off the train from Paris at Victoria Station. And yes, a skinny young

Englishman helped me lift my suitcase off the rack. I remember now the way he watched me with an unfathomable English emotion, when I struck out on my own into the crowd of pale, quick Londoners, who knew where they were going, who understood the money, and who looked to the right when they crossed streets. I understood nothing, barely the language. But there were posters up everywhere advertising the arrival of a Hollywood movie, *Irma la Douce*. 'Irma is coming,' they said.

3

Elephant and Castle

Upon entering London nose-first in 1963, the odours I found
were not pissy or ill-masked by fake gardenia the way they are in
the under parts of Paris, nor were they aggressively mouth-
watering like New York's bubbling oils and sugar. In a few years,
London was going to dust itself off and shake itself down and get
ready to make love, not war, but when I walked the streets in those
early days, trying to get the hang of the place, there wasn't a whiff
of patchouli, just wet wool and river mud, coal smoke, boiled
greens, and under them all, setting the beat, was a puzzling base-
note which for the life of me I could not place. Sometimes, in the
East End or south of the river, a strain of the old air drifts out of a
doorway or trails behind a pensioner on his way to the post office.
When I arrived in London, I was still too young and too American
to recognise the less flamboyant forms of courage. I have learned
to know it as the smell of making do, of shortages and absences, of
fear grown tiresome, of cellars suddenly open to the sky: of post
war in an indomitable city.

The threadbare seediness of my bed-sitter in Kendal Street
gave evidence of a fall on hard times that was as curious and novel
to the child of an upwardly mobile young country, as suet
puddings, salad cream, warm beer, and corner shops where fox-
faced men in raincoats bought cigarettes one at a time. The
building itself had been restored outside to about the height of a

man too lazy or too frail to use a ladder; above a wavering six-foot mark its Georgian frontage was pitted and stained. Over the threshold, in a miasma of cabbage and small dogs, the hall was striped on the one hand, floral on the other, except up near the top where two or three layers of wallpaper had peeled to show a greenish flock in a fleur-de-lis pattern, and no doubt under that, and that, and that, lay hidden strata back to bare plaster. The bottom half of a grand oak tall-boy had been dragooned into service as the front desk; on it was a heavy old black telephone, a big glass ashtray, and a chipped faience vase of peacock blue filled with spears of furled new daffodils. From a perch behind the desk, a dreadful parrot watched over the business. Just as I decided no living creature could maintain such unblinking malevolence and it must be stuffed, the head swivelled my way and let out a dire screech that made me jump. At the door under a brass sign, 'Lounge', appeared an elderly woman – a typical spinster judging from her dress, cut high and ruffled at the throat in a way that managed to be dowdy and kittenish at the same time. Reluctant heiress to a little bit of property and masses of propriety, I thought, and she was still a tiny bit hopeful, poor faded blossom, or why the pearls and kiss-curls?

'Now there's one who has always depended on the kindness of strangers,' I thought. My dentist, Mr Rabin, who unknown to me was at that very moment just setting up practice across the street, told me the other day while he was repairing my crumbling old tooth, that what my Broadway sensibility interpreted one way, nurtured on Tennessee Williams' hysterical virgins, was in fact the London contrary: my landlady had seen out four husbands by the time I'd arrived, one of them not quite her own, and was known locally as 'the merry widow'.

For £2 8s 6d a week, which at the time was around ten dollars, I rented the only one of the eight rooms still available. It was on the top floor, facing the back. She wouldn't help me up with my bag, if I didn't mind.

'Eloise is likely to give birth at any moment, you see,' she told me with the perfect confidence of an eccentric that nothing she could say would be beyond ordinary comprehension. 'You're a Yank,' she called after me as I was climbing the stairs. 'How jolly!'

My window looked out at the back on to row after row of Victorian chimney-pots, ranked like old soldiers, marching towards the bare branches of trees in a neighbouring square. Hardly a block from Oxford Street, the view was nevertheless barely urban, except for the ragged and reckless race of pigeons that infest central London and strut through every frame as if they own it. When we tenants bumped into each other on the stairs or outside the bathrooms we talked about the weather in our various accents; nobody ever mentioned the ghostly patter, it could have been mice, coming every night from lost corners of drawing-rooms that had been partitioned like egg boxes into our bed-sitters: more beds than sitters – big beds, too, that sagged under rough mattresses always slightly damp, and left only narrow walkways to call a room.

Everything that functioned for comfort required money: the heater, a big old radio, an electric cooking ring, and if I recall correctly, even the lights needed an investment of the heavy coins that soon frayed the lining of my wallet, and were as indecipherable in my hand as Egyptian scarabs. I wrote in a letter to Rhoda that to come back every night to the hungry appliances in my bed-sit was like trying to keep house in a bowl of piranha fish. Every time the hissing blue flame of the heater leapt to a match held at arm's length, it embodied the mean comfort – discomfort, really – about London back then that an American was bound to find particularly striking. Paris in retrospect seemed extravagant and wasteful. As I always forgot to put aside shillings and half-crowns for the blasted gas fire, practically every night when it spluttered to the end of my initial investment, I had to decide whether or not it was worth going down three flights and out into the rain to ask at a pub for change. Usually, it was easier simply to creep between the chilly sheets and call it a day. The coins themselves I recollect now with more than nostalgia, with a touch of genuine grief for their lost weight and charm, and for the short-lived triumph of having mastered them at last. The half-crown, the three-penny – say 'thrupenny' – bit, the sixpence or 'tanner', and the wily shilling that turned a common pound into a guinea: to learn their street names and re-school my counting reflex from tens to twelves was the first stage of belonging in London, and I was proud to have done it. When in the throes of decimalisation the government announced the withdrawal of the jolly, jolly sixpence, there was such a noisy public outcry that it had to be reprieved. As soon as the furore had cooled down, and everyone was distracted by the next crisis, the legendary coin was polished off heartlessly, and practically overnight to forestall sentimental obituaries.

The English turned out to be more outlandish than the French, and much funnier, and in ways that continue to surprise me. London was less like an American city than any I'd known, or have known since. Two of my three acquaintances in England at that time were a married couple perpetually on the point of divorce over his infidelities of which, in the strictest sense, I had briefly been one, and an Anglo-Argentinian journalist called Lillian Davidson who had grown up next door to Douglas in Buenos Aires. Lil had been living in London for two or three years. Somewhere along the line Douglas told her about me and gave me her telephone number, but because I wasn't yet ready to talk about him, or perhaps because I still longed to, I put off calling her. Instead I decided to buy a newspaper and scour the ads for a job. To choose a newspaper in London, I found out when I stood for the first time before a rack of them, was no simple undertaking. Londoners have a serious relationship with their daily papers. Freewheeling though your average Londoner's evening entertainment may be, he is not about to transfer his intimate morning attention from the paper of his choice, which is why even now morning television is a flop in England unless it addresses itself to children who are not yet committed to a paper, or to illiterates. A Londoner does not simply buy his daily paper, or subscribe to it; he marries it. His choice of a newspaper says a lot about his status, his ambitions, his taste in political and even sexual ways. He who is reading the *Sun* on the Central Line, for example, and he who is coming off the Hammersmith flyover with the *Telegraph* beside him on the front seat of his Range Rover, are as far apart in spirit as any two urban men can be. That's why many more papers are required here than in any other capital city: ten dailies at the last count, one in the evening, and nine on Sunday. He who does *The Times* crossword probably did not attend the same university as he who does the *Guardian*'s crossword, and if he's doing the crossword in the *Telegraph*, the chances are he's an outdoorsy type with a cleric in the family. The moment a newspaper prints anything that deviates from its established gospel, its readers first probably write letters of complaint to the editor – they most certainly will if they are *The Times* readers – and only after supreme insult will they bitterly and critically sever all ties and shop around for a new voice in the morning. Every English newspaper has a history and a life-span: when they die it is slowly, as a rule, and quite horribly. One symptom of an ailing broadsheet is an increase in stories about the Royals. After that, its advertising slides downmarket, it changes the layout of its front page, and finally it slips away quietly in its sleep, unlike the tabloids that die in noisy fits. Three important morning papers, one evening tabloid, and one Sunday have passed away during my decades here, and two more are fading now. Reading an English paper is something like supporting a football team: an impassioned form of mateyness – the sort of thing blokes like to do. Most of the idiosyncrasies of London life – newspaper addiction, curry houses, betting-shops on every high street, pubs, clubs, Speakers' Corner, Saville Row, marathons instead of floats and parades, the noisy last night of the Proms at the Albert Hall – derive from the sorts of things blokes like to do. Paris has the soul of a thwarted woman; each new disclosure showed me that London is the model of a self-indulgent male.

When I arrived here, the front page of *The Times* was still composed entirely of small ads, giving it Victorian charm, I thought, and I liked the Kiplingesque ring to the sobriquet: 'The Thunderer'. Its Help Wanted ads, however, were of not much use to me. A lot of them were practically unintelligible: what kind of clerk didn't work in a shop? What did solicitors do? What was a Lyon's Corner House? The only possible employment I found in *The Times* for someone like me was with the American Playboy outfit which was opening a London installation. They were advertising for editorial assistants, not bunnies, more's the pity. But the moment I walked into the Park Lane hotel suite for the interview, I could tell from the way the smug Bostonian from *Playboy* looked at my legs, that I wasn't the girl for the job. Eloise, the pekinese, had eventually had her pups very late the night before – the excitement had kept the whole house up for hours, and I was groggy from lack of sleep which made me look more bedraggled than usual. Barely had I begun embroidering my work experience at the *US Army Times* in Paris, when the *Playboy* playboy stopped me in mid-sentence. A flashy blonde had appeared out of what was presumably the bedroom.

'Hiya, doll,' he said.

Believe it or not, even playboys from Boston used to talk that way in those dark days. He didn't introduce us or get up. She kissed the top of his head, and asked in a tweety-pie voice for money: '. . . to buy a pair of shoes'. When I saw him peel five tenners out of his wallet, I knew I could write our meeting off as far as my employment was concerned: he was giving her nearly twice as much per foot as my job would have paid per week.

With the bottom of the barrel in sight, I finally telephoned Lillian. Her voice on the phone was unaccented, light, very clear and belonged in a dainty casing, thus, the first time I saw Lillian, her size came as a shock. In the 1960s obesity was so unusual you could have cruised around London or Paris for months without encountering anyone half her size. Even in the streets of mid-western American cities you'd probably not bump into more than one or two people a week of her mammoth proportions. She was not simply large or plump or big-boned, she was literally off the domestic scale. She seemed to lack all objectivity about her own size and appearance. Once, years after we'd met and become friends, I was asked on a press trip to Moscow, and when I complained of having no coat for the Russian winter, she immediately offered me her gigantic sheepskin tent. Did she worry about what it cost her heart to service the continent of Lillian? Did she know? We never discussed her weight in so many words, a glandular disturbance was the tacit explanation, and she was not seen to eat more at table than I or others; if anything she ate rather less. When the time finally came to move out of my bed-sit into a flat of my own, Lil offered to drive me. While she talked to my landlady about pekineses and puppies, I went ahead to put a case of books into her car. As I didn't want to scratch her upholstery, I opened the boot and found it was already packed practically to the top with empty coke bottles, plastic forks, sticky cardboard cups, greasy papers, and wrappers from candy bars. I slammed the door closed again fast and never told her what I'd seen. Of course, Lillian did not walk, not if she could help it, and during her peak periods of overweight to have taken public transport would have presented practical problems. In the many years I was to be her friend, she had a series of cars, usually sporty numbers that fitted around her like hip-baths. Eventually the springs used to give way under the driver's seat, and sooner or later all her cars began to list, to starboard in London, then after she moved to Paris, they listed to port. Lil could be a nifty driver, and very aggressive. Frustrated agility and anger were liberated only in her car, as was her appetite. From the moment Lil and I met, I felt towards her the exasperated, half-embarrassed love one feels for a very fat child; for her part, she found our friendship novel: 'You're the only straight woman friend I've ever had.'

Until the first time Lil stood before me, I had assumed that she and Douglas had been childhood sweethearts in Buenos Aires; as it turned out, it was his sister she had loved to the point of madness. Lil's eyes were wet with tears when she told me about the scandal it caused in her quarter of the city when she was fifteen and impassioned love-letters she sent from boarding school fell into the hands of both mothers. She looked away from me into the middle distance and a couple of men at the bar turned away hastily before she saw them staring. We'd met at a nondescript pub in west London, one of an international collection of pubs and restaurants Lil endorsed over the years where the food was unexceptional, even disgusting, but where she felt comfortable because the people who ran them were used to her girth, and most of them happened also to be homosexual.

Barely two days after our first meeting, the phone in the hall rang, and the pretty Portuguese girl down the hall had to knock on my door for a change to say it was for me.

'Kurtz,' said Lil. Like Hank and Rho and several close friends to come she had started immediately calling me by my surname. 'I've got you a job with me at the COI. You'll love it.'

Lillian wrote radio and television scripts in Spanish for Britain's Central Office of Information to broadcast in South and Central America.

'A propagandist, Lil?' I asked.

'A journalist,' she corrected me sternly.

Lil was as proud of her English press-card as any 1950s cub reporter, and as confident of its magic influence. She'd shown it to me the first time we met, taking it carefully out of a wallet that bulged with identity cards of every sort, as well as three passports: Argentinian, Uruguayan and British. Lil wrote the kind of innocuous tourist fodder for the COI that I had written for the *Army Times*, not a thrilling prospect. But the man to whom I'd let my room in Paris was being slow with his rent, and I wasn't going to be able to feed all the hungry little mouths in my bed-sitter much longer without some sort of employment. So I thanked her and jumped at the job. I soon discovered that in the office my friend became the bossy fat kid, the playground autocrat and I-must-be-mama, who knew what was best for others and organised them pitilessly. Co-workers found her out of step with the laid-back way Londoners go to the office, they kept out of her way as much as possible, and it was in a spirit of mischief that her department at the COI elected her to represent them in the National Union of Journalists. It was a thankless post nobody but Lil would have taken on for love or money. A retrograde fluke of semantics gave her the title: FOC – Father of the Chapel.

I reported late my first day at the COI, having managed to tangle myself up in the public transport system. London is no easy town for a landlubber to get around in. There is no uptown, midtown or downtown, and barely any right or left. Ask a Londoner at Marble Arch, say, how to get to the British Museum and he'll tell you to go east along Oxford Street, then north at Tottenham Court Road, and indicate the distances not in blocks, as a New Yorker would, or stop–lights, but in minutes: ten minutes east, then three, maybe four, minutes north. As long as winds are fair, skiff and veteran square rigger should make landfall at more or less the same time, and on that principle a Londoner's estimates are the same for a kid on roller-blades or a little old woman pulling a shopping trolley. The postal codes have a maritime ring to them, too, that say a whole lot about the people who live in them. When I arrived in London trendy liberals went from NW1 to NW8, for instance, E1 and other due east areas were eccentric for the middle classes but have since become charming in spots and original; SW1, 3 and 7 north of the river were old-fashioned posh and thus attracted the nouveaux riches, otherwise the SWs were pretty much beyond the pale, except for Battersea in SW11 where raffish enclaves of journalists, architects and similar arty fringe types were starting to be found about the time I settled in London; and so on, and on, through all the compass points and combinations of them.

A lot of London that lies south of the river was bombed to smithereens during the blitz and rebuilt in haste without any architectural distinction whatsoever. Granted, the southern river-bank is lit by Shakespearean glories and offers one of London's moodiest walks; inland too there are surviving streets and crescents of style, in many of them live solicitors, serious writers, accountants and small publishers who were caught on the bottom rung of the ladder when the inflated property market folded in the late 1980s. On the whole, however, London South and South-east are gritty and tough, as famous for villainy as anything else, and in parts seem a different city from the one on the opposite shore of the Thames.

'Oh, no, I don't see much of them anymore,' I overheard my landlady telling a friend on the phone, 'not since they moved south of the river . . .'

The Central Office of Information was in an outstandingly ugly building at the intersection of major roads called Elephant and Castle in south-east London. Common theory holds Elephant and Castle to be a mispronunciation of 'Infanta of Castille' dating back to when she was engaged to Charles I, and to be sure, it's the kind of word-play English has always gone in for. But London is as picked over by historians as New York is by songwriters, and most of them seem to think Elephant and Castle is a reference to medieval heraldry, or to a chess piece. As royal marriages have always been moves on the board of state, possibly they are all correct. I recently passed through Elephant and Castle for the first time in years. Apparently the local council had decided that the place couldn't look any worse, and they'd tarted it up fancifully, with statues of bright pink elephants surmounting the entrances to the shopping precinct. The area was pulverised by German bombs and not put back together again until the early 1960s, just a little while before I came blinking out of the underground one sodden spring morning for my first day at work.

We in the overseas division of the COI shared a big open-plan room where my desk was right in front of Lillian. I was supposed to be writing a short film script explaining the British electoral system to Canadian schoolchildren; a foolhardy undertaking for someone who had never seen a film script and had herself been in Britain for not much more than 25 minutes. I can't imagine what Lil had said to make them hire me, I can only imagine that she kept on saying it, until they gave in. There was a good library in the building where under the umbrella of learning about film scripts and electoral systems I read whatever took my fancy, and there too I wrote long letters to Rhoda that skirted around my congenital bouts of depression, and made the most of London's cunning charm. Although where I worked was a colourless, functional part of town, at the end of my first week I had come upon a thriving street market, the Cut, that was the first sign I'd had of a vivid, noisy life in tandem with the dignity of grander streets. I tried to persuade Lil to join me at lunch-time and sample the raving hawkers and Dickensian tingle of criminality in the Cut. But Lilian never went out for lunch. Just grabbed a sandwich at her desk. I, on the other hand, took every chance coming to me to escape the office.

Lil was deaf and blind to London's local colour. A polemic had begun that was to last throughout my long friendship in which I took London's part against her choice of Paris as the best city on earth. She spoke excellent French and it had always been her dream to live in Paris as she imagined Paris to be: free and tolerant, and full of free, tolerant cancan dancers. But not long after we met, Lillian's widowed mother, Angelica, set out from Argentina to come and live with her daughter. Angelica wanted Lil to stay in London because there, at what she took to be the source of universal decorum, she hoped her problem child would at last stay out of trouble, and whatever Angelica wanted, she got, except of course, a daughter who was a credit to her. Angelica was petite, straight and stiff: the kind of woman who is proud of her china and other small things. It was hard to imagine her having given birth to a baby who had grown to the size of Lil; they seemed a different species.

'A rhino wriggling out of a crow,' was what my gay friend from university, Donald, said after he met them.

When Angelica was introduced to me by her daughter, she turned away from my hand with an explosion of Spanish that was astounding from a woman half my weight and a sixth of her daughter's. Only after Lil explained that I had been a girlfriend of the indisputably heterosexual Douglas, and it was he who had brought us together, did her mother calm down and pat the place next to her where she wanted me to sit. In her perpetual mourning for Lillian's father, with her hair pulled up high on her head and black eyes darting everywhere, she reminded me of an outsized Spanish exclamation mark, quivering on the sofa. They were in the process of leaving Lil's old flat in west London for a bigger place in the suburbs, and we were surrounded by packing cases. On one of them that was serving as a coffee-table was a silver frame containing the photograph of a broad-shouldered man on a horse. Angelica sighed dramatically when she saw me looking at it.

'My beloved house-bound,' she said.

Lil told me later that her mother took the framed photograph with her everywhere, spoke to it and questioned it, and sometimes heard it answer.

'Please, Ear-muff,' Angelica whispered when her daughter had gone into the kitchen, 'tell Lillian to wear dark colours. Yes? She's not too old. Maybe if she looked smaller . . . ?'

Her eyes stopped darting for a moment and fixed on a stubborn dream: *her obese lesbian daughter was starting fresh in London and finding some kind of husband.* Lillian handed around cups of tea and for a moment the two women looked straight at each other. Angelica's dreamy expression changed to contemptuous anger. The old woman knew she had all the force of right on her side. Lil flushed and turned away; on a deep level of helpless guilt, she had to agree with her mother. They were not evenly matched, not until a few years later when Lillian bought a west highland terrier puppy and instructed him so efficiently in anger that when Angelica tried to win him over with chocolate, he bit her hand to the bone.

One quiet day at work, I asked Lil if she had been to America. She told me she was constantly worried that she might be sent over there on a story, because she had lived in New York, yes, and she was forbidden ever to return to the States. She had been caught and arrested for writing bad cheques while trying to impress a Broadway chorus girl from Des Moines. She spoke offhandedly and with sneaky amusement, as if about a childhood prank that had got a little out of hand, until she got to the part where Angelica flew up from Buenos Aires to pull strings to get her off the charge. She was finally released into her mother's custody and with the proviso she leave America for ever. Otherwise, Lil would have gone to prison for a long time. As it was, she spent some months on remand at the women's jail in Greenwich Village. A boyfriend of mine at Columbia had a flat that overlooked it. Who knows? Perhaps she was one of the hefty lasses we used to watch playing volleyball on their fenced-in roof while Elvis sang 'Heartbreak Hotel' on the turn-table behind us. According to the speaking photograph, a terminal crisis in the health of Lillian's father was brought on by shock over her peccadillo. By this time Lil's eyes were filled with tears. Of course she would never enjoy London the way I did: she was in her mother's custody, and London was her jail.

Most Friday nights when Angelica thought Lil had to work late, she was in fact at a gay women's club she'd homed in on at Notting Hill Gate. Occasionally I went along as her cover vis-à-vis her mother, and out of curiosity. Lil swaggered into that funky basement, stood drinks for everyone at the bar, fed the juke-box and lowered her usual tone for laughing, 'Ho-ho-ho!', like a big, butch Santa Claus.

'She's with me,' Lil said, squint-eyed, when a circulating crop-headed gal looked my way.

Naturally it wasn't long before she fell in love. Brigitte was a solemn young French au pair who turned up at the gay club one Saturday, wearing her long hair in two straw-coloured plaits and looking as wholesome as a pantomime Dutch girl. Love and the rights of ownership exacerbated Lil's bossiness.

'Bibiche,' she'd say, sternly, waggling her plump forefinger: 'Stop that. That isn't done here. You're in London now. The English don't dunk their bread in the salad dressing.'

Brigitte smiled at me and sketched a wink over Lil's shoulder. 'That's because the English don't know how to eat.'

Brigitte was too good of heart to encourage any criminal or suicidal extravagances in the name of love. Vaguely, she was affectionate towards Lil whose size probably precluded sex even in private, or much more than the massive cuddles in which she sometime enfolded Brigitte right there at the bar. Long, long after Brigitte had to go back home to provincial France, Lil continued to carry the torch. It was seven years later, before she finally wrote Brigitte out of her will, after she'd heard from her brother in France that his sister had joined a closed order of Carmelite nuns.

Meanwhile, a chill London spring had seeped on into a damp summer and autumn. Leaves on London trees yellow on the branch, then they dry and fall without a fuss. I scuffed them underfoot in Hyde Park, trying not to think about the defiant last blaze of deciduous trees where I came from. Wherever an American east-coaster finds herself, October will contain shreds of ineluctable homesickness. Oh, once in a great while, London comes up with a day nearly as crisp as October in New York; it only makes me hunger for the real McCoy. Generally, autumn brings a steady dose of typical London rain, fine and permeating, like the classic wet squib. In October and November, even footballers and burglars don't leave home in London without a brolly. But people who expatriate themselves to Marbella, say, or Tangiers, or anywhere to avoid bad weather are quitters at their core, just as people who choose to live in a place because it's great for raising children turn out to be bores. We expats to London on the other hand, if I do say so myself, are energetic, interesting and not lacking in determination.

Somehow, by the middle of October I had cobbled together a script about general elections and passed it upstairs. Whether it met with approval and was eventually inflicted on Canadian schoolchildren I never learned, for my term of employment with the COI was over. I packed up from my desk the few things that were my own and yes, it was I, I admit it now, I was the one who spirited out of the Ladies' Room a dozen rolls of stiff, unyielding toilet-paper that was stamped in blue letters on each segment: OHMS (On Her Majesty's Service). At the last minute my departure was postponed by Lillian who had to make a short film on an international show of home furnishings at the Olympia Exhibition Hall, and asked if I would play a South American visitor to London.

'You see her as a mute, boss?' I asked. 'Because my Spanish is nowhere.'

'I'll do the talking,' she said. 'You only have to comb your hair, wear some high heels, we'll rent you a mink, and you'll look the part.'

Time has tended to fade me. When I was young and vivid, in Rome, Naples, Madrid or whatever southern city I found myself, tourists used to stop me for directions. Spanish and Italian men, Israelis, even Turks, ogled when I walked through their home towns, but by reflex they never touched or hooted or hissed; they assumed I was one of their own and would give them hell. Or tell their mothers. My short stunning career in movies, like my street allure, was based entirely on mistaken identity. In fact, Lil's ten-minute documentary was neither my film debut, nor my first experience of miscasting. Two years earlier in Paris, the only American lover I was ever going to have (as far as I know or remember) an ex-Marine and left-over poet from the GI Bill, invited me to Pamplona for the annual running of the bulls and the bullfights. Orson Welles happened to be there that year, and from my cheap seat in the sun I watched him up front in the shade, elbows on his knees, chin cradled between his hands. His concentration had the density of stone. He moved his head once to follow the wilting waxen face of a wounded torero as they were carrying him through the gate of the arena, and once again he looked up suddenly, sweeping his gaze across the stands. I felt it pass like one of those hot winds with romantic names, and for an instant I saw myself: long hair falling to the left in a lop-sided pony-tail; striped matelot shirt I'd bought when *Stormsvalla* was in Cannes; a chunky bracelet that Douglas had made for me – he said its green stone contained 'the seed of an emerald'. I was untidy, adventurous, embryonic, but nowhere yet. As we were leaving the bullring a wild-eyed young man made a determined way through the crowds straight to me.

'Excusez-moi, mademoiselle. . . .'

Would I be an extra in a scene for Orson Welles's film of *Don Quixote* which was being shot that evening in the main square? Mr Welles, it seems, had picked me out himself as the 'French peasant type' he wanted. All I had to do was sit at a table with Akim Tamiroff and drink red wine. Directions came via underlings, but Welles himself could be seen rumbling around the sidelines, and I almost met him. Thus began my film career, pretty much as it ended, with a mistake.

It was on that trip to Pamplona I came across a thin, dark Englishman. We barely spoke, no more than a little joke in passing. But it was he, a year or so later, when my stint at the COI had ended, who was going to give my London life a shove, some would say straight into the gutter, although the locale is more commonly known among Londoners as 'The Street of Shame'.

4

Fleet Street

Journalism is to England as bullfighting is to Spain: a daring national sport that offers youngsters with the guts for it a chance to pull themselves up out of pedestrian destinies. Hopeful scribblers from the English-speaking world are drawn to London the way hopeful toreros are to the Spanish capitals, and good-looking actors to Los Angeles. Only in London does print journalism remain a route to fame and fortune for a few, and a pretty fair income for others. It is not true, by the by, that in every London journalist's bottom drawer are stashed three chapters of an unfinished novel; more likely it's a pile of threatening letters from the Inland Revenue. Most Fleet Street journalists would not be writers in France, for instance, where tacit censorship is prevalent and there are far fewer pages to fill every morning; or if they lived in the vastness of America, dominated by television and lacking national papers. With a less print-hungry public to satisfy, all but a few of Fleet Street's battery would probably be teachers, ad agents, managers of small businesses, bars and cafés or maybe they'd practise law. Some of them would be eventual bankrupts, boring the pants off their fellow bar-flies with boasts of triumphs in the past. Megalomania, once upon a time pretty much an exclusively male condition, now appears like lung cancer and heart failure increasingly among working females too, and especially we London hackettes as we grow older show a predisposition to displays of diseased self-importance every bit as gruesome as those of our male colleagues. Fleet Street is no longer what it was when I arrived in London; the great buildings remain, but they are now merely façades for foreign banks. The dismantling of Fleet Street was accomplished in the 1980s, not quite 500 years after Wynkyn de Worde set up the first of the presses that were to inspire its fame and infamy. Any day now 'Fleet Street' will lapse from common usage as a metaphor for the Fourth Estate, which is itself a venerable epithet for the body of British journalists composed of men and women who are in the main infinitely more credulous than cynical, and much more inclined than the average Londoner to believe everything they read in their papers.

When Fleet Street began to break up and disseminate itself around outlying quarters of London, it so happened I was writing a weekly column for the city's only evening paper. Not much of a paper. Not much of a column. But my son was in a very expensive school at the time, and I was grateful to the friendly editor who put me up for the job. I used to deliver my copy by hand every Wednesday. From home to Fleet Street became one of my favourite short walks in London, or in the world. It was a ritual, in fact, rain or shine, that was soon central to the performance of the week. Along the top of Covent Garden, or diagonally across the piazza where I snootily brushed through the tourists, then over Kingsway into Remnant Street, just a scrap of a block that leads straight to Lincoln's Inn Fields. Long ago the square there was a place of execution and later, in the eighteenth century, it was dangerous to cross on account of thieves who lurked in its shadows. Barristers and solicitors from the surrounding chambers lurk there now for a smoke, and sometimes they use the square as a short-cut to the courts. One November morning a covey of them in wigs and robes crossed my path like an animated cartoon off the pages of an early *Punch* hoofing it into the chilly haze. Even after all these years similar images of easy glamour leap out of the mundane in London so I find myself like a long-time married woman surprised and rejuvenated by a glimpse of the elegant young chap my other half used to be.

Bell Yard brought me quickest from Lincoln's Inn into Fleet Street just within the precincts of the City, at a point where London starts to be nowhere more handsome and intriguing. Samuel Johnson felt so close, I almost met him.

'This is London,' I'd say to myself, 'I have business in London. I know where I am in London.'

Usually in Fleet Street I'd bump into colleagues or chums, recognise celebrated faces, and frequently find myself being greeted by a stranger. As I grow older, strangers increasingly turn out to be people I used to know. Rarely if ever did I take the lift up to see my editor; when I dropped off my copy with the receptionist at the front desk, he always told me what he'd thought of my last column, where I'd gone wrong, and how I could do better. After that, the route home was straight up the Strand, then past St Martin-in-the-Fields, and it was never so delicious because already I'd have begun to worry about how to fill the next chasm under my by-line. Writing a column in a London paper is like sprinting. Except for a few old champions who do a nostalgic lap of honour week after week, it's a youngsters' game. By the time I had a column to write, I was no longer green enough to believe my daily life held parables for the masses; nor was I old enough yet to repeat myself without shame.

Then one day my employers had a modem delivered to my flat with instructions that hereafter all copy was to be filed down the telephone lines. Finished was the purposeful walk. Farewell, pit-stops at the zany Soane Museum in Lincoln's Inn Fields. Bye-bye, dear Doctor Johnson. So long, chance encounters, and gone the gossip of old friends who popped up in my path. In no time, the noble trade of printing that had laid Fleet Street's cornerstone was practically defunct. Adieu, Fleet Street. My paper and all the others moved away into designer office-buildings where the conditioned air contained no resonance of cellar presses, no boozy profanities, no reek of fags, stale beer and ink.

I landed in Fleet Street early on in my London life, pretty

much by accident. Strictly speaking, I guess I was illegally employed in those days, unless my work could have been justified by requiring what Lillian and a lot of Londoners back then in the early 60s called 'American know-how'.

'Know how to do what exactly, Lillian?'

'Know how to make things happen, Kurtz.'

'Like what things, Lil?'

'Things, Kurtz. You know. Razzmatazz . . . and . . . I don't know . . . things.'

When my job with the COI ended, I'd had to make an expensive trip back to France so my visitor's visa could be renewed, and only about ten pounds sterling stood between me and penury. My chronology of this period is hazy, and the journals I kept are no help at all.

'You know your trouble?' Donald used to chide me. 'You're too rational.'

The stronger is a girl's attraction to chaos, the more rational she needs to be, or appear to be, I guess. My old journals are so chaotic and unlike anything I've written for print, I have to find used ticket stubs or clippings tucked into them if I want to pin them down by date. And by the way, who was the neurasthenic sex-crazed gloom-bunny of those journals? I don't know the woman. Her maunderings on madness and despair are Greek to me. She had to go. Her disordered sensibility alarms and mortifies me now, like one of the faces I can't place who confronts me suddenly in a crowd: 'Kurtz, long time no see. I say, Irma, how's life treating you?' It was 1964 or it could have been '65 when the train bringing me back from my duty trip to Paris pulled into Victoria Station. This time, according to my undated journal, it felt almost like a homecoming: I slipped straight into formation with the natives, shoulder to shoulder, looked right when crossing the street, couldn't wait to buy a daily paper. A nice cuppa tea was going to go down well after all the Parisian plonk. 'Oi!' and 'Bob's your uncle.'

A few days later with my passport endorsed again and ready to look for a job, I went out for a Saturday afternoon drink in Soho with an Englishman I knew, a fallen pillar of the community who had recently moved lock, stock and barrel to Ibiza. For a solid hour he'd been moaning about London and decrying everything from its women to its beer. Clearly, he was trying to justify expatriation to a perpetual holiday in Spain; was he too thick to see that for himself and change his tack? He was getting on my nerves. But he was a good-looking specimen, there was no denying it, and I was feeling lonely.

'Stop drinking,' I warned myself, 'before he starts to look even better.'

Suddenly, at the far side of the noisy pub there rose a big sheet of white cardboard and on it in bold letters hastily inked I saw my own name. I recognised the man holding it over the heads of the crowd. Ted Simon and I had met and talked briefly in Pamplona. Kinship drew us together, I see that now, though I wouldn't have said so at the time. Ted was skinny, tall and dark; a sheen on his olive skin made him look as if he were always just coming from an oriental bath. He was not Welsh, I think. Hank had taught me how to play against Ted's superior saucy style with women, and who could resist the original way he paged me across the pub? But he wasn't a comfortable man to be with, not for me, and there was never a romantic or physical attraction between us. Ted fell in love with blue-eyed people who were not awfully bright, and so did I. He was bored with his life, bored at work, bored with London, and too, too bored with his prospects. Boredom made Ted elusive, and I wouldn't be surprised if boredom also made him inadvertently cruel in the clinch. He and a partner ran a small public relations firm out of an office in Fleet Street, and the impulsive, careless way Ted offered me a job, within two drinks of our meeting in the pub, as good as told me how much that bored him, too.

'We could use some American know-how,' he said, 'to complement our own British know-who . . .'

Like a lot of Londoners at that time, Ted was attracted to

America in the boyish heroic way that Australia attracts some of them now. One fair Sunday afternoon a few months after we met, he dragooned a half-hearted gaggle of Englishmen into a baseball game in the park opposite his terraced house, and afterwards I met his young Scandinavian wife. Men whose secret fantasies are chivalric always attach themselves to unusually beautiful women, whose ribbons they imagine themselves wearing proudly into battle. But there were conflicting romances at Ted's table: the tea his pretty wife prepared for us of hand-buttered bread and lumpy cakes was homely and motherly, not courtly, and whenever she looked at her husband, clouds dimmed her baby blues.

I was around 29 back then, Ted was in his early thirties. People over 40 look pretty much the same to anyone in her twenties and whether his partner, Connor Walsh, was 45 or 55 I couldn't tell you. Con had worked on an illustrated feature-paper called *Picture Post* that had gone under in the late 1950s after a highly respected run of over 30 years. From what I could tell his job had been in the production department and not especially glamorous. But *Picture Post* had mythical status in Fleet Street for having published without interruption throughout the war, and its glory rubbed off on everyone who worked for it. Ted deferred to the veteran of a Fleet Street legend and showed him respect that would have surprised his wife, so free was it of his usual mocking overtone.

Ambitious north country journalists like Connor used to head for Fleet Street as soon as they outgrew their local papers, and many of them prospered in the big time, especially in editorial and administrative positions. Northerners were attuned to the populist swing pushing into politics at that time; their respect had to be earned, awe was not in their vocabulary, except as a sneaking reverence for Fleet Street itself. Most of them were shy around women and had got themselves hitched early on to home-town girls. Their marriages did not always flourish in London's southern climate, and to be sure, there was marital rubble way back in Connor's past. For the past few years he had been living with a shrewd, unvarnished lass from Yorkshire, considerably younger than he, and whenever he said her name, 'Boonty', his face could not stop itself reflecting love. Connor knew as much about publicity as I did about cricket, and cared marginally less. Our office was in the attic of a shabby building that was part of Fleet Street only by geography, and when he was at his desk under the eaves, he'd look up sometimes frowning like a man who knows that the best of his career, if not most of it, is behind him. He used to answer his phone – 'Connor Walsh, here' – sounding astonished to be he, there, of all damn places. Probably, Con was at a financial low like mine when Ted roped him in. Ted himself couldn't have been much better off: we had one client.

The divine lunacy of immigrant Celts, in particular the Irish, who carry the sharpest tongues in the English language, gives England's capital a broad streak of satire and surreal wit. About the time I went to work for Ted's company, which was magnificently called 'Europress, Ltd', London had started buzzing over irreverent comic reviews springing up in basement theatres and small clubs around town. The name of the club our client owned was Raymond's Revuebar, naturally I took him for one of the new breed of entrepreneurs in what was beginning to be called 'Underground London'. On my second or third morning at the job, before I'd sorted out what I was supposed to be doing in an office where there really was nothing much to do, Connor asked me to sit in on a performance at the Revuebar that very night and write a press-release about a rising young star in the show.

'Is it underground?' I asked him.

'Underground?' He looked at me curiously. 'No, it's ground level.'

'Is she French?' I asked when I saw that the name of the new headliner was Gigi L'Amour.

'I doubt it,' he said.

I'm not thick. I cannot believe I hadn't caught on before I turned up at the Revuebar. But I honestly do not recall realising until I was nose to nose with the glossy photographs in the lobby of the Revuebar, that what our client ran was a strip-club. The show I'd come to write about, though not a satirical review in the strictest sense, was a parody of Paris, where strip-tease was a suave and sexless spectacle. Visible goose bumps on the Revuebar girls and the way they leered down at the front rows instead of upwardly communing, made the London show dirtier and more voyeuristic than one someone had taken me to once at the Crazy Horse in Paris: it was more 'underground', too, in a fungal way. Backstage, the communal dressing-room was crowded with naked and half-naked women putting on make-up, or taking it off, in front of mirrors with snapshots of babies tucked into the frames. The air was thick with perfumed sweat and cigarette smoke. Gigi L'Amour's real name turned out to be Myrtle Crockett. She was a former hairdresser from Balham, where her folks owned a fish and chip shop. They were not bothered by the way their only daughter made a living; her boyfriend wasn't awfully keen on it though.

'What does he do, er, Myrtle?'

'He's a solicitor's clerk.'

She leaned into the mirror to apply dark purple lipstick.

'Look, honey,' she said between kissing sounds at her reflection, 'why don't you just make it all up? You're probably better at that kind of thing than me.'

In the corridor on my way out I nearly collided with a big fair-haired man wearing an open shirt and flickering gold. Clearly he was our client Paul Raymond. I slipped past while he was talking to a group of minions. Having come out dressed for underground satire, in jeans and a bomber jacket, I didn't feel up to the appraisal of a gent with his evident standards of chic. Feminism was only a glint in mama's eye, you understand, when I was PR for a strip club. Anyhow, I'd been a waitress in Manhattan, and the strip-tease business didn't seem to me all that debasing of women, though I'll grant it didn't flatter men. Myrtle and her cohorts had immense power over their audience, and they wielded it with the nonchalance of great chefs, say, or hired assassins.

Only three weeks after I joined the Fleet Street office, Ted finally persuaded Paul to think bigger than G-strings and nipple-twirlers, to set himself up as London's answer to Hugh Heffner, and became top man of Britain's very own Empire of Erotica that would give American *Playboy* a run for its bright new English shillings. Thus it was, with a convulsive somersault of British amateurism, we ceased to be public relations agents and became overnight the editorial staff of London's first ever girlie magazine. Our contribution to the genre was called *King*. Ted was Editor-in-Chief and Connor was Features Editor: or was it the other way around? As for me, I needed a title too, a minor one, as I was the wrong sex to do much on the staff of a 'stroke magazine'. Ted finally stole my title from the masthead of an American glossy: Merchandising Editor – it made no sense at all, but didn't it sound custom-made for the nudie trade?

Ted anticipated steady traffic of famous contributors and rich advertisers who would find the dark staircase up to our office suggestive of vulgar hanky-panky instead of the 'erotic ethos' he had in mind. The new premises he found were only a block away, and to my relief securely within the Fleet Street mystique. The English journalist who used to drink with me in Paris had been posted back to London, he was showing me the ropes, and I was starting to get the hang of the place.

It isn't true that Londoners drink more than Parisians, though they certainly out-drink New Yorkers. The truth is, Londoners, and the British in general, drink not more, but differently from anyone else. Just the one, or two, or three is simply a part of daily life in London where a life *without* drink – an arid, unsociable, unpunctuated life – really would be a serious matter for nine out of ten Londoners. When it comes to drinking – convivial, noisy, talkative drinking – Londoners are serious drinkers precisely because they do not take it seriously. Once a Londoner starts to drink he no longer counts the cost, not to waistline or lifespan as Americans do, not to his palate, as any Parisian worth his salt does in front of a wine list. He, or she, who does take drinking seriously is inevitably one who takes himself, or herself, seriously too. And due to some fluke of temper or tradition, the taking of oneself seriously is not the done thing in London society. An idio-syncratic *elsewhereness* of ego especially evident in Brits drawn to the capital – their ability to lose themselves bravely, eagerly, suicidally for periods of time – produces great actors among them, and also world-class drinkers. Fill the role, fill the glass: drama is an art-form in London beyond ephemeral entertainment, and so, forgive me, is the dram.

When I landed in Fleet Street, it was a pub-based community. High or low, everyone lunched, and lunches began in a pub; a lot of them finished there, too. Three o'clock was afternoon closing-time for pubs then, and anyone who could then went on to one of the many small private clubs, most of them in Soho, with a dispensation from the licensing laws. For anyone in the know it was easy to drink around the clock in London even before the recent suspension of licensing hours. The bibulous one-upman-ship of knowing obscure after-hours watering-holes increased the drinking pleasure of Fleet Street men. Their thirst had a com-petitive edge that was especially in evidence the morning after when, coffee slopping over their hands, they compared notes on who had emptied how many bottles the night before. Each newspaper laid claim to one of the ancient pubs found in Fleet Street and its narrow tributaries. My friend from Paris worked for a paper that used – and to the fullest – a long pub in Shoe Lane that was dark and mellow and very old. The counter had been rubbed into rills and raised swirls and burnt black chasms; brass door handles and bar fittings moulded by 200 years of continuous use fitted the shape of living hands; ancient nails in benches and chairs showed their heads to the size of a sixpence, and snagged any stuff that came near them: everything there was being softly worn away, including the drinkers. I used to belly up to the bar with the boys and before long I too found myself swept up into the genius of erosion.

A celebrated cartoonist was being courted by Ted to work for *King*, and sometimes after their meetings, he used to invite me for a tipple at El Vino, a more-than-pub but not-quite-club near the top of Fleet Street. There, the editors and leader-writers and other luminaries drank. Assiduously. Women were not permitted to pay for drinks, a custom I found perfectly charming. When a mob of feminists stormed El Vino in the mid-1970s demanding their right to pay, honourable memory prevented me from joining them, for I'd stood my rounds in the plebeian pubs, and it was a relief to be spared them in the toffs' bar. My escort to El Vino was Austrian-born and looked very old to me: 50 at least. When he was a young man, he'd narrowly escaped from his homeland as it was collapsing around him, and he never again had reason to go back. The caricatures that made him well known in London were scathing to the breed of politicians who once upon a time in another country had torn him and his family up at the roots and thrown them away. He said little, just let me chatter away, a talk doodler compulsively filling in silences, as usual: 'Look, look, look, oh, get a load of that one, the silvery one at the bar. See him? So tailored, so distinguished, ain't he? But when he passed, did you smell the mould and stale sweat? There's a man who's proud to make a bottle of shampoo last a year. Baths are too sensual for him, don't you know? Too effeminate for ageing Head Boys. So classically educated. So aristocratically unwashed. So classically, aristocratically, mouldy, sweaty old school . . .'

For moments he brightened to hear me burble over a scene which for him was only a little better than nothing, and in the end, not even that. One day a few years after he and I drifted apart for the last time outside El Vino, I read in the morning paper that he had killed himself. Even though his people and mine generations ago may have started out together on the road, his London lap on the journey was the contrary of my own: mine was set underway by curiosity and hope, two of the great naïve American virtues and about all we have to be getting on with. A continental refugee like my friend, however, when he left his homeland already knew too much and remembered everything: London for him was a dead end.

King started out on top of the world: new premises, a staff of keen newcomers and a few jaded old pros who were only marking time, they'd have you know, until the *Observer* or *The Times* sent for them. For our very first cover Ted and Con wanted an alluring, up-market girl, someone with more 'je ne sais quoi' than Gigi L'Amour from Balham, ready and willing though she and all the Revuebar's strippers were to serve. In the end, Ted decided that his brand new editorial assistant filled the bill perfectly. She was a stunning brunette, pale skinned, slender, demure and elegant. Not an inch of skin below her swanlike neck showed in the cover shot, and there were no nudie pix of her inside, either. She was not that kind of girl. She was the kind of girl any smart man would be proud to marry. In fact, it wasn't long before a smart member of our staff did just that for a while.

As the days went by Ted and Con took longer and longer lunches and set up ever more grandiose schemes involving sports car manufacturers and men who ran casinos. We published superior cartoons and some pretty good writing. Top-drawer readers could have found what they were looking for in *King*, had they bothered to look, but there was very little of what top-shelf browsers wanted: raunchy, naughty, messy old sex. When the Englishmen gathered around the light-box to look at transparencies of nudes for the next issue, whatever might have been their voluptuous fantasies at home, they were as cool and lordly as brain surgeons. For all Ted's hopeful talk of an 'erotic ethos', there really is no more mystery to a girlie magazine than to a cookery book, it's equally functional, and the user always has all necessary ingredients to hand.

Meanwhile, my London was shrinking to a manageable size. Oxford Circus, High Street Kensington, Holborn, Embankment, Baker Street, West Hampstead, the Angel: I could have told you from a seat in the Underground what the streets looked like overhead and at Sloane Square, Mansion House, Notting Hill Gate, given you a shrewd idea how the pedestrians topside were dressed and whether they were there for fun or business. In Fleet

Street, in the pubs of Soho and Chelsea, I began bumping into Londoners who called me by name. Not just our cities shrink, the world itself becomes a tighter fit in time; everyone is bound to leave a smaller place than the one he toddled into. So when somebody mentioned that my old friend Donald had quit his copy-writing job in New York and was living in London, I wasn't all that surprised. The last time I'd seen Donald, while I was working in the fashion trade in New York, I'd said or done something that made him very angry, never hard to do. Before we'd had time to make up the quarrel, only a few days after the slam of his door behind me and the crash against it of a Baccarat crystal tumbler, I left America. Don-Don was like many homosexual men, predisposed to the company of women for everything but sex; he was affable, even loving, when we met again in London.

Lil had finished her contract with the COI and had been employed by a news agency to oversee their Latin American dispatches. She rang me at the office one day in a state of high excitement: she had organised a 'freebie' trip for herself and two other journalists – would I like to come along? It was early spring, the weather in London was foul, and a jaunt to Rio de Janeiro would have been nice, or even better one to the provocatively elongated coast of Chile. Returning from hitchhiking to Istanbul with Hank and Rhoda, I'd lost my way in Venice one memorable night in the company of a Chilean poet.

'Brazil? Santiago?' I asked.

'Denmark,' she said. 'And don't forget your press card.'

Donald and Lil got on very well, so he came too. He was writing copy for a London ad agency and strictly speaking no candidate for a press trip except in Britain where journalism stretched to include all kinds of inky waifs and strays. Copenhagen is a mild and civilised city that received us with the utmost courtesy. No Danish heads turned when Lil strode into town like Falstaff out of the wrong play. From art museums to the Cherry Heering distillery, wherever we were taken by our guides, small chairs were discretely changed for big ones before she sat down, and someone made a speech in awfully good English to welcome us while platters of smorgasbord were toted out with little Union Jacks stuck into the pickled herrings. Lillian put earnest questions one after another to our hosts; Donald drank steadily; I pretended to take notes about Danish politics, Danish social services, Danish economy and the role of bacon in it, though the truth was, anything my *King* readers cared to know, I'd already gleaned in good English from a taxi driver. Because Lil's size made air travel problematical and she was not happy to be separated for long from her car, we had travelled to Denmark by ship. Our passage home from Hamlet's land was smooth, especially for Donald who never left the bar, not even after the Scandinavian sailors had come up one by one from the bowels of the ship to marvel at his intake of akvavit. When British customs told him he was a bottle over his allowance, he broke open the extra one on the spot and chug-a-lugged most of it before anyone could stop him.

'It's lucky for you,' he told the astounded official who tried to stop him, 'that in me you see before you a Cambridge educated poet and not one of your football hooligans.'

The *King* I'd left a short week earlier was not the *King* I came back to. Nobody was at the switchboard, nobody was making Monday morning coffee, there was no noisy music from the art department, no freelance hack with his feet on the desk lighting up his third or fourth cigarette of the day, no beautiful editorial assistants: there was Ted in his office and Connor in his, and a few other people sitting around, and there I was, and nobody else. While I was in Denmark, Paul had pulled the plug. Ted said he was confident he could find backing elsewhere. Would I mind working without salary until he did? It was only a matter of time. And, oh yes, if it wasn't too much to ask, would I please answer the telephones, too?

'*King* magazine,' I said as usual, when the phone rang two Mondays after my return from Denmark. 'Can I help you?'

When I worked for Hubert de Givenchy I'd accidentally (more or less) picked up an extension when Jacqueline Kennedy was talking on the telephone, and now I was hearing her voice again – 'May I speak to Ted Simon, please?' – only the accent was different. It was a voice without pitch or intensity, breathy and childlike, yet devoid of laughter: the voice of a hard man's moll – a victim's voice. Marilyn Monroe had it too.

'May I ask who's calling?'

The previous year, Great Britain's Secretary of State for War, John Profumo, had resigned after he was caught out lying in the House of Commons over allegations that he cavorted with prostitutes. The named girls were Mandy Rice-Davies and Christine Keeler, and they instantly became celebrities. Naturally, it wasn't the blatant blonde, Mandy, but the relatively austere and sensitive brunette, Christine, whom Ted had been courting for a photo feature, and thus it happened that practically the last words I heard in the offices of *King* were spoken by one of British history's good-time girls, for it was Christine Keeler on the line. She had agreed at last to be tastefully photographed for *King* – too late. After weeks without any salaries paid, the cupboard was bare. I told Ted I had to leave.

'I don't blame you,' he said.

One of the hopeful misconceptions that *King* took down with it when it sank was that the readers of girlie magazines actually read. Books often arrived in the office, sent by credulous publishers for us to review. On my way out, after the barest of farewells, I slipped into my bag a collection of Japanese prints that showed couples fornicating athletically in welters of brocaded silks, while from the corners of each frame, woodland creatures – squirrels, owls, chipmunks, rabbits – watched them and tittered, much as the British public does over sex in high places. Desperate for rent-money as always, I steeled my courage to sell the book a few days later in a Soho porn shop. Inside the curtained door to the street was a curiously sedate atmosphere, as quiet as any public library. The man behind the counter was lumpy and pock-marked, only his hands were smooth, and he turned the pages with exquisite care.

'It's beautiful. Cor, innit beautiful? So delicate. Look at that! What can I say? It's gorgeous.' He sighed and pronounced the words that stand in my memory as *King*'s epitaph. 'Trouble is, it just isn't dirty enough.'

King survived my departure by a matter of a few weeks. Some of the people attached to it drifted in and out of my London life for years to come. I don't know what became of Connor. Twenty years or more ago I read somewhere that Ted was setting out to ride around the world on a Harley Davidson. In due course he published a very good book about the journey; I was sent a copy to review. The last I heard, he was divorced and living in a California dream-pit at the extreme edge of the western world.

5

Chelsea

Memory sweeps things under the carpet so the place looks tidy when guests drop by. The era neatly stowed as 'The Swinging 60s', for instance, didn't get started until nearly midway through the decade, and only faded away a few years into the 1970s. It was London that provided the centrifugal force for what turned out to be a world-wide movement, and within London, Chelsea is where the swinging began, with a leap of joy to mark the end of Britain's long convalescence at last after the worst war in the world, one which the English fought with a heart more whole and steadfast than any other Europeans, though it's not considered sporting in England to say as much. The trait that sets the English apart from practically every other western nation is not their head for schoolboy jollification and hard drink, nor their yen for unruly sex, nor even the tattered banner of fair play which they carry on their obsessive quest for justice; it is the English appetite for self-denigration. 'Typical innit?' is the Londoner's weary reply to every new scandal or disaster from a mad cow in Dorset to gerry-mandering in Westminster, as if these islands had a monopoly on greed and stupidity, as if anyone else did it better, as if Britain were not, in spite of it all, the least cynical and grossly corrupt of nations in its league. Expatriates like me, no matter how long we remain at the rock-face, or what papers we carry, can never become trusty Londoners because by our very choice of residence we declare a preference for this city above all others, and to come out and say London is terrific sounds mildly treasonable nowadays.

'You mean you actually like it here?' asks the cabbie, way past incredulity, as good as telling the American in the back-seat she must be off her trolley.

During my early days here I used to think London's almost oriental self-effacement derived from a classic fear of tempting providence with which I could easily sympathise. But as the years passed, so also did vestiges of the greatest empire in the history of the world fall away, and the immense power held by this small island on the planet was gradually given up to its heirs. Until about the time my son was born, all England's proud sway had passed into legend. A trawl through any London department store or the Underground or a crowded street even now is sprinkled with tiny apologies – 'sorry', 'sorry', 'sorry' – sorry about pirates, sorry about slaves, sorry about India, Africa, Hong Kong, Singapore, so sorry about that fiasco in Boston Bay, sorry about meaning well, sorry about driving on the left, sorry about this language of ours that continues to encircle the globe in wit and glory upon which the sun will never set. It's a contradictory mix of self-denigration with shreds of hubris, and it comes out like grudging apology – for what? For having imposed an empire? For having surrendered it? To love the capital is to accept its apology without altogether understanding why. God knows the world would be better off with less chauvinism in evidence and its absence is generally endearing. Nevertheless, national modesty is also practically un-American, and particularly for Yanks in London it needs a lot more getting used to than warm beer and fish knives. Every time I find myself needing again to defend the good things here to Londoners themselves – from the quality of local broadcasting, to the relative safety in the Underground, to the sweeping urban luxury of Hyde Park – then, even after three decades, I know myself to be a stranger in the city I traded for home.

Chelsea was an intact and affluent quarter of the city when I settled there, replete with pubs and gardens, and arty in a comfortable Royal Academy way, not like Soho, say, where writers and painters have always thrown in their lot with low life. There was a rarefied feeling about Chelsea that I've heard American visitors call 'quintessentially London', though it looked more like a prosperous village in Cambridgeshire to me. Thanks to a minor domestic incident, I was signing the papers on a flat off the King's Road in Chelsea the very moment London began to swing. It began one evening in the middle of spring, when I returned as usual to the boarding-house in Kendal Street, disheartened and woozy from clinging to the wreckage of *King* for another day. The cleaner had come that morning, she did every month or so, and a stinging smell of bleach hit me when I opened my door. Like nine out of ten windows waiting for me in future London homes, the one in my bed-sit could not resist gravity; she had left it open on its own, and done what she could to prevent the sash from sliding down. I had very few possessions at that time, and the only one of any distinction was a fifteenth-century Greek icon bought while Hank and Rho and I were hitch-hiking across Europe.

After two cheap, elegant months in a Moorish watch-tower on the Mallorcan coast, we weren't ready yet to let summer go. Why should we? So we had started out on foot from Barcelona to Istanbul. While waiting for lifts on ancient roads overgrown with brambles and wild flowers, Hank and I performed like a pair of gypsy clowns to keep Rhoda from falling ill or despondent. If the car or cart or caravan or truck that pulled up eventually had room for only two of us, Rhoda and I left Hank on his own to catch us up later. I'd look back and see him standing on an unknown road, the lucky vagabond, free to put one foot in front of the other and discover the turning globe independently, awkwardly, all alone, like a stubborn child. 'Pon my soul, if I'd been a bloke, you wouldn't have found me travelling with Rho, or with me, or with anyone. Rho and I had arrived in a small village just over the

Greek border where Hank had caught up with us the night before, as he always managed to do. It was a glorious sunny morning and we were on our way out of town when we came upon a man seated on a straight-backed kitchen chair by the side of the road. A piece of whitewashed wood lay on his lap and he was bent low, painting on it. Pots of bright paints stood on the ground at his feet, and chunks of dark wood were scattered around him which when we came closer we saw were antique icons. As we watched he daubed quickly over the whitewash, following the visible outline of the original in Woolworth pinks and blues, so he could end up with a swanky Madonna like those we'd seen being sold next to melons in the market. Hank poured enough drachmas into the hands of the bemused artist to rescue several large icons, and a wonderful small triptych I had spotted deepened by centuries of incense showing Christ's entry into Jerusalem. He presented it to Rhoda. Three dollars I could spare secured an icon of the Virgin and Child. It was damaged, but the faces rose clear out of the wood and the pale entwined fingers were pointing the way: to London and 56 Draycott Place in swinging Chelsea, as it turned out. The moment I saw that the cleaner had taken it down from its hook on the wall and used it to prop open the window, I knew it was time to move.

I had been drinking to the memory of *King* in a Soho pub with a seven-foot-tall Scottish sculptor, and when I started incidentally complaining about my bed-sit, he told me his former girlfriend was going back to the country to marry a 'poxy squire . . .' by which I took him to mean a member of the landed gentry, and her flat was coming free. I didn't yet know enough about London to be impressed by the fashionable Chelsea address he scribbled on the inside of an empty cigarette packet but the rent of £8 a week for a one-bedroom flat was affordable, as a new job was already lined up, thanks to my friend Donald, with the ad agency where he worked. On the spot I telephoned the number the Scot gave me and arranged with his ex-girlfriend to view the place right away. The Victorian building it was in looked very like what New Yorkers call brownstone, except it was of red brick. Stairs rose from the pavement to a handsome front door flanked by window-boxes planted identically with ivy and geraniums. Clearly it was a house well-tended, if not loved, and had been all its life. The ex-girlfriend's flat was on the very top, an attic, and the moment I saw it, I knew it was perfect for me. The young woman at the door was a big lassie, inflated further by the overweening heartiness that girls from good families are taught in English boarding-schools, and use as a way to crush underlings.

'Hallo, hallo, hallo. Awfully nice of you to come . . . so glad . . . so glad . . .' she said, chivvying me into an overstuffed chair, and: 'Sit!'

She was a potter, she told me, and I was glad when she said the flat came unfurnished and without the lop-sided pots on every flat surface. It was sunny, self-contained, adorable, and I was ready to take it over on the spot except first she said I had to be vetted by a representative of the Cadogan Estate to which the property belonged. No sooner said than she was on the phone to 'the Colonel', making a high-pitched appointment for him to meet me the next day at his home.

'Right-o, then, Colonel . . . Hands across the sea sort of thing . . . American cousins sort of thing and whatever . . . How absolutely sweet.'

Having no firsthand idea yet of the ways love took the English upper classes, I wondered if excitement about the landed gentleman accounted for her giddy telephone manner. Looking back later I realised that to foist an exotic like me on to the Cadogan Estate was one last act of rebellion by a faint-hearted bohemian on her way back home.

The next afternoon, there was I, in the Colonel's drawing-room, gripping a bone-china cup of china tea and overlooked by portraits gone in craquelure. Outside the french windows, barely discernible through the trees of Cadogan Square, I could just make out the bulk of another building equal in size and middle-class pretensions to the one we were in. It belonged to the posh prep school to which years later I was going to 'bus' my son from a far less salubrious part of London; and though I did not know any such thing at the time, that must be why whenever I now try to summon the Colonel of Cadogan Square into my mind's eye, the headmaster of Sussex House will pop up instead. I can't recall if the two men looked alike; they certainly looked at me in the same way. The colonel was asking himself what kind of name ends in 'Z'? His suspicion that I might not be top-drawer didn't worry me in the slightest: snobbery is a two-way road, and I am not that kind of snob. Besides, expats are exempt from local class systems, discounting, of course, those English Catholics and High Anglicans who take their faith as a social class to which only the blessed and the blessed only belong. To be honest, if divisions must be made, I can see an argument for grounds of birth rather than money: class can be copied, but not stolen, and throughout history heads have rolled for being high born, which hardly ever happens to people with too much money. Parisians would kill to have a royal family in residence again; as things are, they produce no world-class gossip for export. Without Royals and their attendants as a home-grown source of pomp and melodrama, London might have to rely altogether on imported gossip from Hollywood the way Paris and practically every other city does. Peeking up the skirts and trouser legs of overlords and keeping them under scrutiny helps us keep tabs on where we stand in relationship to each other and our society: gossip is a glue of community – it's our answer to dream-time and story-telling. And upper classes are a whole lot easier to take than movie stars: at least they're allowed to grow old in public these days, and they generally have better manners than movie stars. Admittedly, some are criminals and plenty of them are nincompoops, but very few are hypocrites and it's not often they are mawkish or as egregiously sentimental as most movie stars. Gross ambition can't drive them: what were the poor things born for, except to be gossip fodder? The best of the bluebloods therefore show a little humility and a sense of grievous destiny altogether missing from movie stars and other self-made big shots.

'Delightful young woman, isn't she?' said the Colonel. 'Have you known her for long, Miss-ah-um-Coutts?'

Local snobs sometimes soothe their misgivings by taking my name – Kurtz – for that of the Queen's bankers: Coutts. Similarly, a Ku-Klux-Klansman I interviewed once in a Louisiana bayou, giving me the benefit of the doubt, insisted on hearing my name as 'Curtis', and I did not put him right, either.

'Yonks,' I replied brazenly. 'Known her for yonks. Simply ages and ages, actually . . .' Noblesse oblige. I'd come to the Colonel recommended by a girl with an excellent hyphen. What could he do but accept me? Neither the Colonel nor I knew that even as he was deciding to grant me my two-year lease on a bit of the Cadogan Estate, the pendulum had begun its forward swing, and in merely a few months his sort of snob was going to have to hole up in the country while hairdressers and photographers danced down the King's Road, Chelsea, with princesses in their arms. The sad thing is that from the start the poor old Colonel was confident at least that an American ending in 'Z' would be okay for the money. Over the years countless messages of restrained despair and disappointment arrived from him every time I was late with the rent yet again. After I finally decided to leave Chelsea, I sent him Rhoda as my successor. Her secretive nature gave her a protective colouring in some circles of London society much more effective than my own, and she had by then reverted to her maiden name, Edwards, an anglicisation I'm sure of something that had ended in 'Z'.

Youth had been a condition not considered good for much beyond war and sex, until suddenly in the 1960s it started to claim a 'culture' of its own. Just about the time I moved into my new flat young people were becoming a market force, particularly evident in well-heeled areas like Chelsea. At weekends, hardly any grown-ups were to be seen abroad in the main shopping street, the King's Road, only the Chelsea Pensioners, outstanding in scarlet ceremonial dress of a design that dated back to the eighteenth

century. One special bunch of girls stood out in the neighbourhood then; later, I heard them called 'Sloane Rangers' after
their Chelsea purlieu. They treated the top of the number 19 bus
as a sort of morning club and I used to study them out of the
corner of my eye on my way to work while overhead rang their
tree-top screeches, the tribal voice of young Englishwomen born
and bred to marry well. The tube is considered by Londoners a
more manly way to get around – buses are for girls and old ladies
– so I used to see the male counterparts of the Sloanes, known as
'Hooray Henrys', only when I happened to take the Underground
to work. Unlike their womanfolk they were very well tailored;
their hair was beautifully cut to fall across the brow. As a rule they
had narrow eyes and thin lips; they were slender, lecherous,
superior. Most of them sounded thick as two bricks, and they
were all scared to death of foreign brunettes.

Had I denied wanderlust and remained in America, I would
probably have been finding grounds for my first divorce at just
about the age I moved to Chelsea. It turned out to be a good thing
that I never saw the point of marriage. The further a lone woman
goes from home and the longer she stays away, the more she
reduces her chances of finding a husband. Men by and large are
curious about foreign women and keen to have sex with them.
The fact remains, however, that a young London man-about-
town is no more imaginative when it comes to the girl he takes
home to mother than any handsome Greek beach bum in Corfu.
At the end of every academic year, brainy American women
mainly from New York start turning up at private views and publishers' parties, and in the entourage of ageing literary figures;
they are husband-hunting in London. By the time the autumn
rains begin, most of them give up and go home, and one or two
who get lucky have been known to misread the signals so that they
end up with a man who is English, true enough, but not the
Englishman they took him for. Although it was an explosively
flirtatious time for everyone in London who could squeeze under
the flaming bar of 30, none of the new people I met wanted to

settle down. Most evenings after work a bunch of playmates met by appointment or by chance at a friendly pub and then went on to cheap and cheerful restaurants, and two by two, to bed. Of course, I was pretty regularly in love or getting over it; I could not tell you now with whom, only that I meant it at the time, every time.

The age of Aquarius was gleaming on the horizon; even teetotallers in youth-stricken Chelsea, if they were young, were smoking pot. On that very score (in a manner of speaking), I had been arrested with Douglas a few years earlier in Paris. The police who broke into my room on the Île Saint-Louis while we were placidly smoking a joint were armed with sub-machine guns. It was a cold night in January, and wind tore through chinks in the back of the paddy-wagon that took us away. Poor Douglas, it was his birthday, and he was in a state of dark concentration next to me, already willing himself far away from his new year, and Paris, and me. On the bench across from us sat a pair of prostitutes in skin-tight satin that glistened along their lines and creases like the olive oil of a classic French dressing. The short ride to a night court was just another hazard of their trade; they soon lost interest in us and turned away, bored, to watch the city passing like silver ice behind the bars of the window. I felt very calm, and curious. A year or two inside looking out was certainly going to give me a more liberated view than the only one I'd known: being outside, I mean, looking in. There would be no going back after that, and no more charity. It wasn't that I liked the idea of going to jail, but there were interesting dimensions to the possibility. Doing time could do for me what common sense and cowardice prevented otherwise. When all my handicaps had been stripped away – second-rate education, middle-class pretensions, semitic fastidiousness, parental expectations, modesty, innocence – when all I was was gone and all I'd been becoming, then finally I could start to be. What? A real bad hat, maybe. A revolutionary. A beachcomber. A nun. An artist. One thing was sure: Hank was going to envy the shit out of me when he heard I'd gone to jail.

As it turned out, the closest I got to prison that night was a drab olive antechamber where they sat me on a funny sort of electric chair and took my picture from several angles while a young African student of police methods watched and took notes. When I smiled at him, he was shocked and turned away quickly, and I saw a chasm open between me and decent folk. Then I was pushed into another office where Douglas was already waiting and where to my surprise a boss-eyed man who was certainly not Jean-Paul Sartre gave us a court date, and sent us on our way. Because the flat was in my name, they kept my passport and naturally, they kept the plastic bag of dry marijuana plants that we had brought back from a trip to Tangiers with an insouciance that would be unthinkable now. Idiotic as it sounds, we'd had no idea anyone could care that we smoked marijuana. Probably nobody would have cared; we'd been offered up to the police by a friendly Canadian chap who hung around the cafés, and who turned out to be a convicted paedophile. I learned much later that he had been offered his passport back in exchange for us, after he'd persuaded the police that we were the kingpins of a vast drug ring. Suddenly there we were, side by side, outside the police station in the freezing cold. Three months later we were due in court. Meanwhile the phone was bugged and we were followed by plain-clothes policemen for a few weeks, until they got fed up and disappeared. Then a month before we were due in court, Douglas packed up and left for Ibiza with Hank and Rhoda. When the car had pulled away from the street under our window – my window, I mean – I was scared for the first time. Towards the end, Douglas and I had been unusually gentle with each other, and when I turned to face the empty room, mourning still hung in the air.

I was not after all required to tame sharks or keep house in a whale or make revolution and jailhouse art. Common sense touched my life again with its dull magic and the judges in their red robes merely fined me the equivalent of £80, which I had to borrow later from Hank. They also rescinded my permanent *carte de séjour*, requiring me thereafter to renew it every six weeks. My lawyer was a tough *pied noir*, friend of a friend, who thought the whole thing was a joke and a waste of the court's time. Being a good man, he refused a fee. Not long after I'd moved to London, no less than Charles de Gaulle himself declared an amnesty on minor offenders and destroyed existing files, as is customary in France in the wake of an election.

Three years later, I wasn't as worried as I should have been about the crumb of hashish someone gave me in Chelsea that I took with me on a quick trip to Paris to renew my English visitor's visa again. Hank and Rhoda were in the old flat, nothing had changed or been added; the manuscript hadn't grown, but it had reproduced, and there were now three equally high piles of paper next to the typewriter on the desk. The marriage was sunk. They hated each other. They were marking bad time until one of their private mysteries could be resolved: the one about money I think – a way had to be agreed for Rhoda to be supported. The joint I rolled for them ineptly soon after I arrived was the first dope either of them had smoked. Rhoda puffed on it and hummed to herself for a while; claiming it did nothing to her, she suddenly set about one of her paintings with a crimson brush, regretting it next morning. By the time I left them two days later, Hank had turned himself into a master-doper who knew all about weights and provenance, and where to buy the best stuff in Paris. Typical of a man to forget the woman who turned him on in the first place, isn't it? I hope he never remembered. As Don-Don used to say, in the end drugs turn out to be what you take them for. And from the first puff, as Hank began to explode with cosmic revelations, he took his drugs very, very seriously.

I'd never before had such a stylish sort of address as Chelsea, London SW3 was when I moved there. The King's Road was on the very point of turning into a street of fashion: no more than three or four weeks after I moved in, two greengrocers, a butcher and a laundry became shoe-stores overnight. Later, towards the end of the 1970s, chain-stores pushed out most of the boutiques and bistros so they could cash in on tourists who continued to flock there, and still do, in search of the boutiques and bistros. These days the King's Road looks like any other high street with hardly more charm or variety than a suburban mall. I never go back now unless I'm invited by friends who belong to the Chelsea Arts Club. The membership of the Arts Club is by and large as ramshackle and decrepit as the building itself that has sat for a hundred years embracing a glorious garden, with its back to the changing streets. One of my more spectacularly disastrous love affairs was acted out at the Arts Club, and for a while the place was off limits, but every day brings less and less chance of bumping into anyone from the past who remembers, or gives a damn.

The redbrick house I lived in was not as typical of the area at large as cottages swagged in clematis and wisteria to be found on neighbouring streets named after great families of the past and sedate landmarks: manors, ancient trees, churches, chapels. But the roof made cosy corners in my attic rooms just right for shelves of books: tea brewed in an old brown tea-pot; even a cat wasn't out of the question. Most weekends I was happy to bask for hours in the warmth of my own walls, at least until the spectre of another Monday morning at the ad agency rose up to drive me out for escape or oblivion.

Rhoda was my first house-guest in London: or anywhere at all, now I come to think of it. She arrived without Hank to spend my second Chelsea Christmas with me. Donald had known her slightly at university, and he was going to join us for dinner. John Sandoe's wonderful bookstore had survived the rejuvenation of Chelsea, as it would come through the subsequent invasion of the King's Road by chain-stores, too. I bought Rhoda a new collection by Pablo Neruda, one of her favourite poets; is it odd that she gave me the very same book as a Christmas gift? At the time I thought it was a sweet coincidence; now, I wonder if we didn't both buy the book for her. I was going to give Don-Don a highly-praised new translation of (I think it was) Verlaine, by Richard Howard. Donald and Richard had been friends when we were all at Columbia. Then Don-Don won a coveted Kellett Fellowship and left for Clare College, Cambridge. Now he was plugging mine-strone at JWT. I put Richard's work back on the shelf and bought him a new collection of Graham Greene's essays instead.

Outside Sandoe's bookstore, mist around the street lamps cast haloes over us gliding home in the long dusk of London in December. Unlike a lot of my neighbours who shopped for food in other areas, I patronised any local shopkeeper with the guts to hold out against the marauding boutiques. The former butcher's shop was now selling mini-skirts, the dairy was a jewellery shop, there was no more dry-cleaner and the nearest fishmonger was a bus-ride away; one greengrocer, two corner shops and a baker had not yet shown the white flag. What was more, they remained stoical before the onslaught, and unusually uncomplaining for Londoners. In one bag I was carrying the books for my friends and a roll of spangled blue wrapping paper; in the heavier bag were two French loaves, cinnamon, a dozen eggs, ginger root, parsley and three pounds of parsnips. Recipes milled in my head along with warm images of a lit gas-fire upstairs and a whisky from my own bottle. Suddenly, there on my doorstep as I scrambled in my purse for the keys, a waft of heavenly cosiness lifted me and swept me away; it felt as warm and doughy as baking bread, and when it had passed through me all too quickly, it left a sense of purpose and well-being to which I became instantly addicted. I smiled at the dingy winter sky, the pigeons, the red phone box on the corner; I had just been bound to London in a way of which I understood not much more than it was womanly, and for keeps.

As long as I was furnishing my new home and for a while later, what I used to call in letters to Rhoda 'the nameless longing' gave up possession of every cell and retreated to a small place under my rib-cage. Antique shops were far too expensive for my pocket, as well as being smarter than my taste; it was at honest junk shops further afield I found what I liked and could afford for my new flat. People who live alone attach almost supernatural qualities to objects, and every dish or piece of furniture I bought for my Chelsea flat brought with it an omen. The captain's table that a dealer in Bermondsey swore dated from the eighteenth century was so convincingly warped that plates slid straight off on to the carpet, but it also had side-flaps a hostess could raise for a glittering sit-down dinner. True enough, the second-hand sofa was reminiscent of a boring childhood, not one's own, but it was comfy and long enough to serve as a spare bed when some amusing aged personage or a platonic poet missed his last train home after a party. As for the old hospital bed with a crank to raise and lower the head, Lil drove me back from Kilburn with it tied to the top of her car; it was bigger than an ordinary single bed. Unlike a woman, a girl never knows her luck.

I treated myself to a Spanish rush-matted bench from a terrifying chic shop on the border of Chelsea with Pimlico. They delivered it on a Monday morning; I sat on it for my dinner, and afterwards carried it into the bedroom to serve as a bedside table. The following Monday, there was an identical bench wrapped and waiting for me in the hall downstairs. On the next Monday when another one appeared, I wasn't surprised: I'd expected it. A Spanish rush-matted bench turned up yet again on the fourth Monday running. I started toying with the idea of going into the rush-matted bench business for myself, and immediately the spell was broken; they stopped coming. But not before it seemed to me my London life had been touched by a wizard who was nutty as a fruitcake, but not unfriendly.

6

Berkeley Square

In the late 60s a Parisian model I knew stopped over in London on her way back from Los Angeles, and we bumped into each other at a gallery opening. After we'd chatted about nothing much, she asked me to explain what 'funk' meant; she'd heard it praised in America, and she wanted to get some in. I explained about sartorial objets trouvés, and how to let things hang as they fell and fall as they hung, I subjected her to my theory about the kinship between funk and kitsch, told her how to avoid Hawaiian nude lampstands that wiggled, and go instead for calendars that were six or seven years out of date, and finally I suggested if she really wanted to take in the meaning of American 'funk' she'd have to try a marshmallow with-peanut-butter sandwich. 'Look,' I said at last, 'be smart. Give it up. You're a Parisian. Even if I could make you "funky", you'd only turn it into chic.'

Nicole, the young secretary who worked in the *US Army Times* office, was always flat broke even before I was, and long before the end of the month. Like every other young Parisian I knew, she lived rent-free with her parents, and except for buying her own clothes, she had no practical expenses whatsoever – not unless you count an occasional trip to London for an abortion. Near Paddington Station is a cluster of small hotels that used to be full of French girls who arrived pregnant, then went back to Paris a few days later practically virgo intacto. Otherwise, Nicole used to spend a month's salary on a belt, and every centime she earned went on the accumulation piece by piece of a classic wardrobe.

'Qu'est-ce-que tu en penses, Irma?' she'd say, and do a little pirouette in the office. 'C'est chouette, n'est-ce pas? C'est chic . . .'

What she was wearing was indistinguishable from what she'd worn the day before, and it was precisely that perfect sameness and sameness of perfection that showed chic. Nicole's taste would be outdated now; sloppiness is in for the young. Nevertheless, I can always tell which of the student tourist groups in the centre of London are Parisian: they alone are not simply sloppy, they are perfectly sloppy. Young Americans can be sloppy, too, but not so perfectly sloppy as Parisians, and never as chic. Chic is congenital to the women of Paris: they are born with it. Even when Parisian women are naked, they have chic. New Yorkers, on the other hand, and Americans in general, put chic on for special occasions. Only in Paris is it the native dress. As for Londoners, when Nicole's London counterpart splashes out it's going to be on a tight skirt that caught her eye in a shop window; so what if it's shocking pink lurex that does not match or enhance anything in her wardrobe? For a little while at least, it makes her feel good. Londoners do not have chic; they have fun, and for a long, long time not even that.

The ne'er-do-well scion of a grand family, who was a copy-writer at J. Walter Thompson in the mid-6os, invited me to the opera at Glyndebourne. During the interval I watched matrons of his mother's age and younger strolling about the beautiful lawns, dressed in what their generation calls 'gowns' or 'long frocks' that were so lacking in style or joy they could not have been chosen by a sense of fashion but by a sense of right and wrong. These were women who had learned how to dress when vanity and frivolity could not honourably be indulged. The tough priorities of a nation under siege were enshrined in street-length coats of sludgy wool over long peach-coloured frocks that I saw strolling the lawns between acts of *The Magic Flute*. Men of the same age were looking terrific in uniformly well-tailored dinner-jackets.

While mothers and grannies were swanning around the opera in sensible shoes, the young women of London had started to twist and shout all over the place wearing skimpy shift dresses in magenta and lime with their hems above the knee and rising steadily. Mascara became the essential cosmetic, and cobalt-blue eye-shadow, white lipstick, eyeliner as black as a houri's kohl. The first ever London 'look' as it happened in the 1960s wasn't chic and wasn't smart: it was angular, lurid, tarty. And wasn't it fun? Fashion in Paris is a vocation; in New York, it's big business. As for London, if entertainment some day emerges as the main function of human societies – and I honestly believe it could – then funny old Londinium will be ahead of its time; streaks ahead of Los Angeles, say, where entertainment is merely a branch of industry. In London, industry, politics, religion, fashion and practically everything, is a branch of entertainment.

It used to annoy me that after we London movie-goers had paid the price of a West End cinema ticket we were subjected to twenty minutes of advertising before the film began. I've stopped complaining about the ads, however, because nowadays they are as technically accomplished in Britain as feature films, often wittier, and even more moving. But advertising was just getting underway in London in the 1960s; It was run by fogies and timid businessmen, and the agency I went to work for was particularly square. So many second sons of famous and titled fathers were employed by J. Walter Thompson in those days that the whole show had the hierarchical priorities of a priesthood. Applicants to write copy for JWT had to sit a test requiring us among other things to describe a thunderstorm. The test was much more fun than copy-writing turned out to be. Worst of all were the meetings. Thousands of pounds' worth of university education from all over the English-speaking world used to meet for hour after hour to debate, say, whether the small print on a label ought to read 'Campbell Soups, Limited', or dare we drop the final 's', and use 'soup' in the singular? It was my first job with a big international company, I had never known time could be wasted on such a monumental scale. Individuals can make up in their own time for the time they waste; time wasted by a group is gone for keeps. Meetings of more than two people, unless they are called to make war or a party or music, accomplish less than nothing and are barely excusable as democratic rituals. They stroke egos, particularly of those who can call them; all that has ever been concluded at any meeting I've attended is a reaffirmation of the pecking order. In the dreary days before British whimsy took over and turned ads into entertainment, JWT was the meetingest damn place in London outside the Houses of Parliament. Summoned yet again to the account executive's office with my team, I used to sit as close as possible to the window to be nearer the sky, trying to look as if I had the foggiest idea what the others were on about; and as if I cared. Back at the machine, when we drudges had to call the product 'soup' or 'soups', the jargon of the meeting was no help at all. Why not just flip a coin? Agonies of boredom at JWT were such as I'd sworn after university never voluntarily to endure again in this life.

Berkeley Square was just outside our front door, and nobody would have objected if we 'creative staff' had strolled there looking for inspiration. Two hundred years or so ago the buildings around Berkeley Square were lively and splendid, but they had been turned into office buildings, some with car show-rooms on the ground floor. No living soul remembered hearing nightingales sing in Berkeley Square; little warblers did not redeem the place from its hauteur. The oldest plane trees anywhere in London met overhead in traditional dress, too high and mighty to be friendly. Every night long after we plebs had returned to our grubby holes and burrows, the trees decked themselves out in paper lanterns for a secret night-life. That was when the nightingales began to sing, in ragtime, while ghosts in phantom Rolls-Royces were arriving to make the whole place jump with Oxbridge quips, and shimmies, and champagne, and kisses behind the swinging trees, until first light filtered through the branches and whisked them back to nowhere. A few hours later, we working stiffs trooped in to the headachy old square for another humdrum day.

Shepherd Market, only a few blocks west of Berkeley Square, in the early eighteenth century was the site of the May Fair, an annual roister that used to put the wind up the local gentry, and to this day the naughty enclave off ever-so-uppity Curzon Street frisks behind the international hotels of Park Lane and serves as their red-light district. We copywriters didn't go there often for our pub lunches; the danger of not bothering to return ever again to the office from such a jolly location was too great to risk. Usually, we fell into the Red Lion Pub just behind JWT and an oasis in the chilly Mayfair outback. Back at my desk, trying to distil twelve lousy lines about chicken broth out of impatience and confusion, I found myself instead writing something else: a page of my journal, the start of an essay on buying rounds in London pubs, say, or on love, and the occasional swollen sonnet. Hardly any wonder Rhoda in Paris received more letters from me than since my time in New York, or that Don-Don and the rest of us rarely returned completely sober from lunch when there was nothing much to do in the neighbourhood but drink. Exclusive shops nearby in Bond Street were all so far above my pocket they seemed to look down on me as if I were a wretched creeping thing. To window-shop without any hope of a splurge, or even just a bargain, is demeaning; silks and jewels and Italian shoes, untouchable under glass, make a poor wandering American girl think twice about just what she's doing with her youth and her looks. There were casinos, too, and London's most expensive hotels within spitting distance of Berkeley Square. There was money all over the place, and very, very little of it was my own.

The time had come for me to choose a bank. Until then, given the vagaries of my career and its guiding principle of hand to mouth, to open a current account had hardly been worth the trouble. My last current account had been in New York where banks were soaring, vaulted spaces staffed by acolytes of the Dollar supernal. Banking in London turned out to be a much more pastoral affair. In those days banks were managed by men whose chief responsibility was to their flock. Any of us with a special interest in money, or special problems, made it a rule to establish a caring, sharing one-to-one relationships with our bank manager. I never felt securely a part of London life until years after I'd arrived when for the first time I heard myself say: 'Sorry, can't see you at ten. I have an appointment with my bank manager.' To have an appointment with one's bank manager was as good as saying that one's time was beginning to be worth more than one's income, which meant one had expectations great enough to warrant going into debt. The terms of the debt were pretty much up to the bank manager's discretion, and nine times out of ten it was to discuss them one was summoned to meet him. His judgement would be based on one's track record, of course, and who knew one, and whom one convinced him one knew, and perhaps most of all, on his hunch about one's ambition and earning capacity. In the main, it was an honourable system and it worked: I don't recall hearing about more financial scams and scandals back then – it seems to me, there were fewer of them. When a Londoner found a sympathetic bank manager, he stayed with him wherever he was posted, even if it meant moving his account to a distant part of London. For more than 30 years, I stayed with the small Barclays Bank near Berkeley Square where I'd opened my first account. Only last year, after it was absorbed into the vast Park Lane branch, which immediately replaced all vestiges of a bank manager with voice mail, did I finally move my account conveniently nearer home.

Of course, forward-thinking borrowers did not wait to be called to a meeting with their bank managers; they made the appointments themselves, boldly, and when big sums were at stake, they invited the bank manager to lunch. By the 1980s, I'd worked my way up as far as an exchange of Christmas cards, but I never earned enough to take my bank manager to lunch, and now it's forever too late. Technology has changed the nature of banking in London more than any other high-street service, and the old ways have been brought down. Money, always a fairly airy-fairy concept, has gone absolutely abstract: ordinary banking is done on plastic through a hole in the wall, 'personal bankers' who are barely out of their teens sort out problems with their eyes on a computer screen, and since the financial tumult of the 80s, the bank manager has lost his place as top man on a middle-income Londoner's support team. Those who can nowadays afford to run into debt, have replaced the bank manager with someone called a 'financial advisor'. 'I'm taking my financial advisor to lunch' lacks the resonance of lunch with a bank manager and is not a statement of any style.

When a Londoner wanted to make money, chances were it was so he never again needed to think about money, or making money, or think about anything, or making much of anything. As a general rule, the very idea of lots of money – as much as it has always excited Americans – fills the heart of the average Englishman with indolence and idle dreams. A cavalier approach to finance suits me very well: money and I have not much more than a nodding acquaintance; we do not hang around together. I have never got on well with the rich. The only very rich man I fancied possessed a fortune so ancient that it had the patina of an ordinary thing, and was easy to take in one's stride. Going out with him, I discovered that in London the richest places are also the quietest: exclusive men's clubs where you can hear a newspaper unroll in the room next door, murmurously posh restaurants, Sotheby's grand auctions – silent but for indispensable voices, and houses in Hampstead Garden Suburb or the Boltons that are double-glazed and set back from the road. The first thing rich Londoners buy is peace and quiet. I went with my rich lover one time to a casino in Mayfair where the hush would scarcely have oscillated the needle of a sound meter. Because I don't care enough about money to get a kick out of gambling, I tiptoed around watching fortunes pass soundlessly from one pocket to another. At the back of the room were two one-armed bandits that nobody was playing, they were there as a joke, I guess, and without thinking, I threw two half-crowns into one of them while I was passing. I have never been so embarrassed as when my coins hit the jackpot. Heads snapped around to glare at the noisy new money that was clattering out of the slot machine on to the parquet floor.

In November when I'd been at JWT for about six months Rhoda telephoned from Paris to invite herself over to stay with me for Christmas.

'And Hank?'

'Who's Hank?'

Lillian arrived for a drink a few hours after I'd brought Rhoda back to my place from Victoria Station. It was their first meeting and it was not made in heaven. Lil brought her dog, Oberon, a west highland terrier she'd bought when he was no more than a whimpering handful of pedigreed white fur. Full-grown, he turned out to be smaller around that Lillian's forearm, but nobody laughed to see him strutting in her huge shadow; she had reared him herself, maternally and possessively, and he was very dangerous. Oberon sat at the door, growling like an empty stomach, never taking his eyes off Rhoda, who preferred cats at the best of times. When Lil had gone and Rhoda was being supercilious, I tried to explain how from the moment Lil had been born, she had never been able to rely on an easy welcome.

'She grew up where bribery was a valid social contract, that's why whenever she comes to see even a good friend like me, she brings bottles and sweets and all these extravagant goodies.'

Rhoda shrugged: 'She's picked an ugly way to kill herself . . .' she said, and mulled over the box of juicy fruit gums Lillian had brought.

First Rho was going to eat the red ones, then the yellow; she'd leave the green and black; nobody liked green or black fruit gums. Once in Paris I brought a cake to the flat to have after dinner, and while we sat drinking before our meal, Rhoda picked all the glazed cherries off the top of it and ate them one by one. Hank and I both watched her doing it, and when she'd taken the last cherry we exchanged a look of exhausted reason, like the parents of a madly wilful handicapped child.

Except for lovers who came and went like visitors to the fire, and Don-Don with a few of his gay friends, my crowd in London were unmarried women. Maybe I should have thought with more self-interest before I presented Rhoda to the Londoners. My eagerness to introduce friends to each other has always been puppyish and ill-considered. But what the blazes? We all grow to an age where we do not make new friends so easily. None of my lot are as young as we used to be, in other words. And who wants a funeral without mourners? A few days after Rhoda turned up, I gave a party for her. Never stirring from her rush-matted bench piled high with cushions near the heater, like a venerable guest of honour, she engaged separately with the guests, drawing them to her one by one, then dismissing each to make way for the next. As soon as everyone had gone home, she leaned in at the doorway of the kitchen sipping red wine and watching me wash up, while she laid out my new friends for me: the envious vanity of the pretty one, her self-importance and dissatisfaction, the guilt of the redhead, the blonde's dark roots, the big girl's compulsion to have everything anyone else had. Fib, exaggeration, solecism, solipsism, selfish tic, affectation and incipient bitterness: with the narrow aptitude of a doctor in a war zone, Rhoda went right for what hurt. It was grisly. She forced complicity too if only because I knew as soon as she could, she would be talking to the others about me. I'm not sure I ever liked Rhoda. She never liked me, I know; she never liked anyone. But we went back: we had our myths and language, we knew songs the others didn't know, we hated baseball – we were attached. She was my last American.

Rhoda was supposed to return to Paris a few days after New Year. She was killing time in Paris, painting a little – maybe she'd write a book? When Hank finally sold the Paris flat, half the money would be hers and a steady allowance, thereafter.

'I've given him my prime time, Kurtz. Where is this famous novel of his? He's let me down. He owes me.'

Many years earlier, while I was back in New York, Rhoda had taught one term of American History at a posh girls' school in Switzerland. The staff politics upset her, and the students were thick as bricks, and she hadn't worked since. Without Hank and Paris, she would probably have been back at Barnard, an academic who kept a stable of wretched girls in hope and fear. She would never have remained a spinster as most tyrannical schoolteachers do: her sexuality pulled too strong. I'd seen it reel men in past her bad skin and wavering oddly boneless silhouette.

'You'll go back to America then, I guess,' I said. 'You'll be going home?'

My first London cat had recently taken up residence; he was a tabby tom called Sherman, after the tank. Sherman ambled out from under the bed and leapt on my knee. I stroked his purring throat.

'Home?' I thought. 'Home.'

'No, no,' she said, 'I'm never going back home.'

Her vehemence surprised me. Imperceptibly, America had been moving further and further west of everything that sang to me. But Rhoda was different, she had no wanderlust or grit; after a few days without home comforts she went into a sulk.

The morning before Rhoda was supposed to leave London she was very pale and quiet when I left for work. I came home that evening to find her groaning in my bed, not on the sofa, her hair spread out on the pillow, her voice so faint I had to lean close when she asked please, please for a cup of tea. The condition was familiar, Hank and I had been through it with her often enough in Spain and on board *Stormsvalla*. But one of the infectious symptoms of Rhoda's affliction was selective amnesia: at the onset of each attack nobody could remember the last one, so it always arrived as something grave and frightening. One notable bad turn occurred in a poky Turkish town not far from the coast when we were hitch-hiking back to Paris from Istanbul. Donkeys were tethered in the main square, there were two cafés and a single hotel where the water ran brown and thick when we turned the communal tap in the hall outside our rooms. Hank and I were keen to go on the next day a few miles down the road to the site of ancient Troy.

'Rubble!' Rhoda said.

She'd had enough of over-ripe melons for dinner, she told us, and enough of bugs on her pillow, and more than enough of the open road. The time had come, she tightly said, to kiss it all goodbye. To blazes with hitch-hiking or hopping a freighter, as we'd half-planned to do if we could find one going to a convenient port. She wanted hot showers, good wine, clean clothes, cakes with real whipped cream, fresh sheets, and she wanted them now, this very minute, thank you very much. It wasn't that we didn't see her point: we were tired too, and I was running dangerously low on money. But what student of great cities, if they have done their innings on the *Aeneid*, could resist following the road to where the topless towers of Troy had stood once, whole and fabulous?

'We'll put it to a vote,' Hank said.

The vote was two for a detour to Ilium against one for an immediate return to Paris.

'That's not fair,' she said, and went straight into a sulk. Wouldn't speak. Didn't want food. Glared at the old men rattling their beads in the square. Come with us to sigh for a while over the broken walls of Troy, we pleaded, only another day or two on the road, and then we promised to do as she wanted and board the Orient Express straight to Venice and civilisation.

'Okay, Rho? C'mon, Rho. Be a sport, Rho.'

'Not fair,' she said.

The illness struck next morning with the very same symptoms I was seeing in London: lethargy, pallor, thirst, lack of appetite, and soon afterwards a persistent low fever would begin. There was no question that she was genuinely suffering. Pain pulsed visibly at her temples. Her forehead was hot, but when she took the cup of tea her hands were dry and cold. And she would not have a doctor. The episode in Turkey lasted six days while Hank and I shredded our nerves on black coffees and played increasingly homicidal rounds of double solitaire. There was a barn outside the town that served as a cinema where he and I sat on a carpet of sunflower-seed husks among dark men with moustaches, and watched the same movie for six nights running. It starred Victor Mature as a backwoodsman. It was dubbed into Turkish. On the seventh day Rhoda recovered enough for us to catch the train back to Italy, then France. Her London attack lasted precisely the same length of time. It was one week to the day later than originally intended, when I saw her off on the Paris train from Victoria Station.

'Be good, Kurtz,' she said, and 'actually,' she added thoughtfully, 'I rather like London.'

With foreboding I heard her pseudo-English accent.

For a woman in rebellion against common destiny, my early career was ironically mixed up with food and feeding: waitress in Manhattan, sea cook on *Stormsvalla*, tea-maker to porn merchants, purveyor of soup (soups?) to the masses, and finally a few months after Christmas I quit JWT to be employed by a celebrated cook and restaurateur, Robert Carrier. My new boss was an American who had arrived here years earlier in the chorus of *Annie Get Your Gun*. Being of a warm and impulsive nature, he took one look at London and jumped ship. London liked the look of him, too. In his youth he'd been a slender, handsome, blue-eyed fellow with black hair. When Bob and I met at one of Donald's riotous parties, he had already acquired a layer of wholesome fat from eating only the best. When Don-Don and I were together at JWT, Don-Don rented the basement flat of Bob's big house in Gibson Square, Islington. 'Dear old Carrier bag . . .' Donald used to call him.

Before the party was over, Bob offered me a job in a small PR outfit he ran. The pay was no worse than I was making, and it was a ticket out of JWT. I stayed with Bob's company, as it happened, barely a year, long enough to gather my courage for the leap into what would become my good old London milieu, to say nothing of my long-term métier.

7

Islington

One evening at a posh house in Islington, a borough which in the
1970s had started to overtake Hampstead as the venue for
London's bloodiest ritual dinner-parties, I found myself at table
next to a grizzled American academic of some renown. Only a few
years older than I, he had stormed out of our homeland during the
McCarthy era and was often quoted as saying he had no intention
of ever going back. He saw himself as European by affinity, British
by preference, a Londoner by adoption: much as I see myself,
except my choices were not made in anger. It was well known he
was an angry American who wanted nothing to do with his
countrymen unless they were of Nobel stature, and even then he
kept his gloves on. During the long dinner he ignored me until I
said thoughtlessly, more to myself than to him, as I passed the
cream for his gooseberry fool: 'Double your pleasure . . .'

He looked directly at me then, and his blue eyes gleamed
through their old cobwebs.

'Double your fun . . . ?' he said tentatively.

'Doublemint, Doublemint, Doublemint gum!' we sang in
unison.

'Would you walk a mile for a Camel?' he asked. 'Do you wonder
where the yellow went?'

'What do you think has happened to "Mr Keene, Tracer of
Lost Persons"?'

'I don't suppose you remember "pickle in the middle . . ."?'

'Jack Benny. "Allen's Alley"? "Kimo Sabe"?'

' "Hi-ho, Silver!" "Shazam"?'

'Captain Marvel. Do they still have O'Henry bars, I wonder?'

'God, they were tasty,' he said with a downward glance at his gooseberry fool.

'Blueberry bunkers. MacIntosh apples in bushel baskets. Poison ivy. Poison sumac . . .'

'Oh God! Yes. Yes. Can you ever forget humming-birds? Fireflies? Frost that turned your bedroom window into a valentine. Remember? And October. Will you ever forget our eastern October? Armies of pumpkins springing out of the fields . . .'

The Londoners had stopped talking. They had drawn back in their chairs, and they were watching us. We two Yanks smiled at each other; his smile creaked a little, but there was hope for it. Then he sighed, and looking around he addressed the table at large: 'Who knows what evil lurks in the hearts of men?' he asked, shaking his big egghead sadly.

'The Shadow knows,' I whispered to him.

And we nearly fell in love.

Expatriation, as the Americanised execs at JWT would have said, is 'an ongoing process'. Probably a sex change is similarly subject to fits and starts. Even now after more than three decades of living in London there are days when I'm waiting in a queue for a bus in Upper Street, Islington, let's say, and it's inevitably raining; and what do you want to bet I've just crossed half the city to a shop that no longer stocks whatever item I used to buy there: 'Oh no, there's no call for those,' the salesman said, probably adding a cluck of disapproval that I should dare to ask, and naturally, for this *is* London, the bus is twenty minutes overdue. And I look around at the other wretches in the queue because I'm longing for a little commiserating kibbutz. But they turn away from my wild eye. And that's when suddenly I wonder: 'Who are these people? What sunless place is this that they call Lun-dun? How the hell did I wash up in Lun–dun? I am undone in Lun–dun. A stranger and a sojourner here. This city is so far gone in restraint and attic codification it's more like Tokyo at heart than any other western city I know.'

Even the street-crazed don't wave their arms around and call loudly on God the way they do in New York; instead, they shuffle along mumbling, and it is they, the London lunatics, who give us sane ones a wide berth on the pavement. Then just in time, before I start to babble or cry, not one, not two, but three number 28 buses loom on the horizon. The bald girl in front of me in black fake leather pants, high-heeled boots and a ring through her nose turns to me, or maybe it's the old man using his pensioner's pass for free off-peak travel (I keep meaning to go to the post office and apply for mine) who turns and asks: 'Do you know why they always come three at a time?'

I shake my head, no, as if I've not heard the punch-line countless times before.

'Because,' she, or he, or whoever, says loud enough for everyone to hear, and it's all in the delivery: 'they're bloody terrified to travel alone, aren't they? The timorous buggers.'

People laugh and my heart lifts, and then we disperse, sitting far away from one another on the bus, opening our newspapers: true Londoners, too respectful of each other's space to push an old joke beyond its range.

Back in the 1960s, there I was, a foolhardy, moody, unfinished expatriate, full of curiosity, self-doubt and hope, not much changed in fact from long gone days in Jersey City where Donald and I had both been born and disdainfully grew up. Except of course that I was no longer in love with Donald by the time we met again in London. Falling in love with a nervy, literate homosexual was easily done back in the mid-twentieth century by a romantic young virgin who found herself in a town overstocked with louts and budding hooligans. I was never again driven to repeat the phenomenon of falling for a gay man, mind you; only very dissatisfied women are. A woman in love with a homosexual man is being constantly rejected, or always seducing him in spite of himself, and either way reeks of self-loathing. Not that I was alone in fancying Don-Don: back in the 1950s at Columbia, such a number of undergraduates of both sexes were joined in love with him, all we needed were the Greek letters – a psi, a psi again, and how many more psis? – to qualify as a fraternity on campus. People who knew Don-Don only in his querulous middle years would hardly believe how startling and distracting and priapic was his very presence alone or in a crowd when he was young. Cheekbones like little suspension bridges and narrow cunning eyes set slightly askew, his face belonged on a runaway Russian ballet dancer, while his spare, knobbly body had the slightly spastic coordination of a dedicated intellectual, or a sailor on shore leave. Of us all, he was the best read and for a while the best writer, too. Only Don-Don in that place and time possessed a crooked, playful wit that was English in style, though back then we doe-eyed American kids didn't appreciate irony, and we complained to each other that he was cruel.

In the 1950s Donald was working as a fellow at Cambridge University. Between terms at Barnard, on my maiden trip to Britain, I slipped away from my student tour group in damp, grey old London – 'I could never live in this weary burg', I find written in my journal of the time – to visit him in Cambridge. An endless party was going on, well, that was the impression given by the stale air and young men slumped in corners. It was late afternoon and outside the windows of Donald's rooms the River Cam was orange and gold, running along the edge of centuries and through the bones of science, rinsing the soft tissue of how many sainted poets?

'La, la, la!' came Donald's most sardonic voice suddenly. 'I see we are yet again to be subjected to the sunset.'

I turned: it was not Donald after all who had sliced through my reverie – it was a tall Englishman I later came to know well, called Simon Hodgson. Simon died not long ago, too soon, and forever missed. Talking to naughty, darling Simon for the first time, I began to realise that Donald's pawky irreverence, rare though it was among Americans of the day, blended into the ordinary mass at Cambridge. Evidently his ability with hard drink was nothing special there either. And perceptible tremors in the room hinted how thirstily his sexuality was being absorbed too, and probably going for a lot less in such an overheated atmosphere than it was worth at home.

Abroad is death for some very bright people. They are fixed stars, distance dims them and in a little while they burn out, then disappear. Though Don-Don was daring of brain and groin, he turned out to be a stay-at-home at heart, and Cambridge, UK was the beginning of the end of him. At Cambridge Donald's sense of being special, always more fragile than his admirers at home realised, was converted into camp extravagance. When he found it not so easy to impress in this old country as he had back home, he started to imagine that the hyphenated bastards had it in for him, and were joining forces to keep him out of their inner circle and out of print. With every lost engagement of wit, he became increasingly convinced the cold-blooded, lily-livered, English intellectual establishment was out to get him because his alien gifts threatened their pre-eminence. It's a common enough brand of paranoia among American scribblers in London, and believe me, it is not unjustifiable. Nevertheless, in the end, it's our own vanity that drives us crazy. As soon as Donald convinced himself that they wouldn't let him win any glittering prizes, he stopped trying. Eventually, when he was around 50, still writing copy for agencies in London, he chucked it all in to return to America once and for all, to his mother's retirement home in the Florida boondocks. But it was too late. He was a half-baked expatriate: too soft to stick it out abroad, too bitter and crusty to go back to being American.

Islington was a north London slum in the early stages of gentrification in the 1960s, and my new boss, Robert Carrier, the celebrated gourmet and cook, owned a big house in one of its prettiest squares: Gibson Square – 'the Gibson girls', Don–Don used to call Bob's ménage. His own basement flat in Bob's house was bright and airy and not at all what the word 'basement' brings to mind. Were there three of us or four employed by Bob? For the life of me I can't remember. I remember the small office we shared, jerry-built shelves running the length of it, I think it was near the top of the house; I'm sure it faced the garden. Details of this period are hazy not because of drink or drugs; luxury is an opiate too, and five-star memories have the sameness of blood heat. Bob's sensuous gift for luxury is rare enough among men, and it was at a premium in London. To have good taste or a good time among the English has always been a test of stamina. Things have improved slowly over the years, but there are still plenty of freezing corridors in art galleries, crush bars at the opera, queues for loos at theatres, warm beer, spot heaters, and too often even now standard lumpy gravy that belies good cuts of meat.

Paris is a city famed for charm yet practically uncharmable by anything outside its own invention. New York is dazzled by novelty, but competitive and frenetically on the hop, with too much to do to hang around for as long as it takes to be spellbound. London, on the other hand, though it has been battered past being easily impressed, is nevertheless very easily, almost childishly, charmed. It will stop in its tracks for a Canadian circus, say, or an Australian stand-up comic, or an enthusiastic American evangelist, or any other import with the power to beguile. Generally, London behaves very like a man, and, as any woman who has been around will agree, this means that like a man London prefers being seduced to being seductive. Bob was a handsome, charming flirt from the USA who soon had *le tout Londres* eating *brandade de morue* out of his hand. He'd learned to cook when he was young and lovely, while being wined and dined in St Tropez; his style was adapted from the French and jazzed up with merciless lashings of champagne, cognac and cream. When his recipes began appearing all over the place in London, everyone was captivated by their sheer sybaritic chutzpah. Bob was essentially a merry man, and the business of publicising apples and pears, for which he'd set up our small PR office in his house, would have to depress anyone with a heart bigger than a Bramley, so he left that boring stuff pretty much to the three or four of us on his staff. All Bob needed to do was breeze in one door of the office and out the other once a day or so, talking fast and musically in his operatic tenor voice, and we were inspired to work our tails off for British fruits. Meanwhile, he and a few other emergent cooks of the period were having a great time charming England out of its penitential eating habits. Thanks to them, English cuisine, which had for a long time with perfect justification been a worldwide joke, slowly began to shake itself free of clinging limp greens and gravy. Bob's energy and charisma galvanised the domestic staff too, though they were mostly francophone North Africans who didn't always grasp what he was getting at. Ahmed the houseboy, fresh from the Casbah, was often to be seen clutching his forehead and frowning over an order Bob had let fly while he was rushing by. One morning there was Ahmed in the garden under our window, humming to himself and sticking cut long-stemmed red roses in even rows into the turned earth of a border.

'Ahmed,' I called down, 'just what are you doing?'

When Ahmed smiled, his teeth had the tinged whiteness of a bitten Russet apple.

'Mister Carrier, he say to me, "Ahmed," he say, "for summer, I wish you plant roses in the garden." So I am planting roses . . .'

One advantage attaching to a woman, at least while she is young and reasonably attractive, is the chance to lead a high life even while she's worrying sick about the rent money. Every so often Bob used to invite me to a dinner at home with A-list guests, or to a restaurant opening or a private view, and as these occasions always came up at short notice I kept my only party garment on a hook behind the office door. It was a black silk jumpsuit which five years later was going to be instrumental in the seduction of my child's father. Wherever in London Bob and I happened to be, on the stroke of midnight he saw me into a taxi home, and it wasn't my glass slipper in his pocket, or on his mind, as he sauntered off towards the late-night pleasures of London's West End.

Christopher Kinimonth was a published author, temporarily on his uppers, who worked alongside me in the apple and pear division which Bob ran as a sort of orphanage for neglected writers. On cold wet nights in the winter, Christopher and I used to go to a local pub where we sat as near as we could to the window so we could spot the oncoming lights of our separate buses home in good time to run for them. More than once we'd let a bus or two go by in favour of another round of Whisky Macs. The pub we used was on the verge of schizophrenia as it affects long-standing local businesses in parts of London where gentrification sets in. The plebeian dart-board remained as tradition would have it, right next to the Ladies' Room door – they put them there, you know, to make women think twice about popping into the local for a drink with the boys – but it had already taken on the dusted look of an artefact, and no serious game was ever in progress. Like most London pubs in those days, there was still a lounge bar where nice folks paid a few pence more per pint for a genteel atmosphere, and there was the public bar with its own entrance, where men on their own could get roaring drunk and use bad language. These old distinctions went by the board as soon as interlopers like Christopher and me chose to drink in the public bar, not the lounge, on egalitarian principles, and because it was more fun. Gradually the public bar filled up with art editors and their wives who had just moved into the neighbourhood, and the old regulars began to huddle in a shrinking group; a few of them suddenly died, others fell to the staggering prices outsiders were starting to offer for their rundown homes. With their windfalls they bought bungalows in suburban green belts where their grown-up children were already installed, having been unable to afford houses in the upwardly mobile neighbourhoods where they and their ancestors had grown up.

In Paris, unless something is added to the central nervous

system of the city, such as the new opera house near the Bastille, or subtracted from it, the way the inner-city market of Les Halles was not long ago, the use and personality of neighbourhoods are set in stone. A girl from the sixteenth arrondissement now is still the Parisian princess she was 30 years ago; the Left Bank retains bohemian credentials; anyone who lives on the Île Saint-Louis is going to be interesting, anyone who lives in the fifteenth probably isn't. Parisians are scared of their suburbs, for it is there in high-rise buildings that grip the city like a claw they stow their Arab and African immigrants. As for New York, the outer boroughs are a mystery to me: I've only ever been to the Bronx for the zoo. The permutations of where is 'in' and where is 'out' are bound to be limited on a small electrically-charged island like Manhattan. A residential see-saw seems to be at work there: west side, up; east side, down; uptown, oops! downtown, whee! Then practically overnight all change sides. In central London gentrification sprinkles itself around here and there and wherever it sets in, it's there for keeps. Terraces, crescents and squares compose most of the sprawling residential areas of London, and their design succumbs to pockets of infection faster than you can say 'carriage-lamp'.

I recall another Islington dinner-party in the late '6os, when our rich socialist oxymoron of a hostess boasted of how much good she and her husband, a famous journalist, were doing the north London backwater to which they had recently moved.

'We're the thin end of a caring wedge . . .' she said.

These days Islington's Upper Street has gone posh enough so that a hostess in a hurry could shop locally for her dreaded dinner-parties. Back then, the roast on her table certainly did not come from the corner butcher. But who am I to blame early affluent settlers for choosing Harrod's Food Hall over local butcher shops that still smelled in those days of cheap cuts and suet? The local school was a disaster area too; it probably still is. Why shouldn't they have put their infant son down for Eton? There is no logic in my dislike of gentrification. After all, nice

people have to live somewhere too, right? They restore dilapi-
dated properties of real architectural merit. Their advent doesn't
necessarily create such an uneasy 'them' and 'us' condition as I
feel even now in Islington. All I know for sure is that when
Christopher and I went for a drink one night, having not been to
the pub for a while, and found the original dusty lighting replaced
by lamps set in mock wagon-wheels, new ashtrays stamped
'Martini', and an eager young company man from a big brewery
behind the bar instead of the cynical old publican, I knew then
that I didn't like Islington.

Fruit pretty much takes care of itself in the publicity department.
Apart from digging up a few odd recipes and circulating them
around the cooking press, there wasn't a whole lot to do. Once in
a while we'd arrange a competition for new uses of apples and
pears: they had to be culinary, of course. There were photo
sessions to attend for the illustrations of Bob's books, where I
picked up a few useful hints: the best way to put a high gloss on
a turkey, for instance, is with hair-spray, and ice-cream won't
melt under hot lights if it's sculpted out of play-dough. For hours
on end in the office I tapped happily at letters to Rhoda, and I
wrote pieces mostly for my own amusement. Christopher must
have been doing the same thing: his machine was going steadily
too, and he had no more than I or any other normal person has to
say about apples and pears. Finally, on a whim I sent a piece
called 'Love in Capital Cities' to a London women's magazine,
Queen, that years later merged with *Harpers Bazaar*. They
returned it with a letter saying it was too 'idiosyncratic' for their
readership.

'What the hell,' I thought.

I helped myself to another couple of big envelopes from the
supply cupboard, wrote another covering letter on office
stationery, and sent the piece out again, this time to a brand new
publication I'd read for the first time that very morning on the bus
into work. It was a large-format glossy called *Nova*. The piece was

sent on Monday and I put it out of my mind. On Friday morning my phone rang. Maybe I'm romancing but it seems to me in retrospect that the moment Dennis Hackett introduced himself in a north country accent buoyant with energy, I knew he was the man I'd been waiting for. Indeed, Dennis turned out to be one of the three or four most important men in my life. To hear an editor, or *anyone*, say he liked my work made me tongue-tied with embarrassment; it's a miracle that he didn't write me off as a drivelling idiot before the end of our conversation when he said he not only wanted the piece, he wanted me on *Nova*'s staff. Bob never quite forgave me for the speed and excitement with which I left his employ.

On the Sunday before my first day at *Nova* Lillian called me. On principle, Lil preferred to use her phone at work for all private calls, and she so rarely rang at weekends from home that I asked immediately if everything was all right? She told me she had just returned a few hours earlier from a short trip to Ireland with Angelica. They'd shared a cabin on the overnight boat from Cork, and in the small hours of the morning, Lil had been awakened when Angelica jumped on her pounding with her fists and screaming.

'She was yelling that we had to run away. There was a fire in the house. Water from the firemen's hoses had filled the streets, and was streaming down the window.'

All Lil could do was hold her struggling mother and immobilise her until a stewardess, alarmed by all the racket, summoned a doctor who fed Angelica sedatives until she finally stopped screaming and fell asleep.

'She must have been having a bad dream, Lil. That's all it was . . .'

'Do you think so, Kurtz?'

'Sure. Of course. Sure. How is she now?'

'She doesn't remember what happened.'

'See? She woke from a bad dream, saw the sea against the porthole and it scared her. That's all it was.'

Something genuinely promising was starting for me at last. Good times made me too selfish to imagine that something horrible could be about to begin for someone close to me. In any case what could I have done for Lillian? Sometimes the only way to help a friend in trouble is to lie to her.

8

Covent Garden

'I used to know John Lennon,' I told my son's girlfriend. It was in the middle 1980s; we'd not very long before moved into the flat where I'm living now. My boy, Marc, was home on his school holidays and there had been a steady flow of teenagers in and out for days.

She blinked: 'Oh yah?'

Marc rose from where he'd been sitting on the floor. His unwinding height never stops surprising me. He put a disc on the CD player and the speakers in the top corners of the living-room gave forth a terrible sound.

'Brill!' the girl cried. 'That is so brill!'

'Most excellent!' said my son. 'Just listen to this, mum. Broaden your musical tastes.'

Where do they get their nerve, these bold beautiful kids? Where did we get ours? The generations are nations too, fitted out with accents and idiom, music and legends, as well as their own emotional, ideological and material allegiances. Take my coevals and fellow citizens in the land of the 1950s, for example. We pledged allegiance to the flag (locally), Elvis Presley, true love, Hemingway, Dylan Thomas or e e cummings, Juliette Greco, Camus and Gitanes sans filtre. We believed in one man for one woman and happy endings, some of us in Communism, others in God. We thought strapless dresses were swell, so were duck's ass haircuts for boys, and we knew our parents were square (some things never change). In due course we all become expatriates, resident on shrinking islands, hanging on to our precious preferences and allegiances and argot, never mind that their objects have died or been discredited and the zone in which they flourished was long ago trashed by invading waves of young vandals.

'Ow about a cuppa, mum?' asked my son in the accent of his expensively educated generation of Englishmen.

'Yessir, I interviewed John,' I heard myself drone on while I made tea. 'Also John Huston, Jeanne Moreau, Polanski, Twiggy, Mrs Bandaranaike. She kept me waiting while some chap in a robe gave her the morning reading from the entrails of a chicken. Mrs B.,' I said, 'was the head of state in Ceylon . . .'

'Sri Lanka, mum means,' explained my son.

'You know, if we were now in pre-history,' I told them as I removed my spectacles to wipe steam off the lenses, 'I would have taken a wrong turn and fallen off a cliff by this time or blundered into a sabre-tooth tiger.'

I intercepted their high–eyebrow look.

'I met all these famous people, I mean, well, I guess I have to say I nearly met them, when I interviewed them for *Nova*.'

'Oh yah? What's a nova?' the girl asked my son, not me.

'A sort of shooting star,' he told her.

They exchanged another look and a slight shrug. Between the young behind and death dead ahead, is it any wonder that nobody over 40 is sane?

Travellers aren't lucky people. To pack a bag and hit the open road is to emigrate from most of the coincidences and affinities that pass for luck at home. Expatriates and gypsies of all kinds exchange garden-variety luck for unexpected marvels, for serendipity. Before *Nova* I strode around like puss in boots, fulfilling fairy-tale fantasies – falling in love, living on a boat, moving among islands, pretending to be Parisian, strolling across countries – and moving on. It had not happened to me before, and it has not happened since, to walk into the right place at precisely the moment a door was opening to let me in: serendipity. *Nova* magazine was serendipitous, it gave me an unexpected purchase on a life in London. And of course, as any kind of good fortune is two-edged, so serendipity also stopped me cold. After *Nova* was over, I was too deep into London to move on, or want to; my papers had been put in order, I had become a registered alien, a settler and almost complete expatriate.

The initial inspiration for *Nova* came from a talkative, skinny, ebullient, classically and expensively dressed redhead, already in her middle age, Alma Birk, later Baroness Birk of Regent's Park. I suspect that when Alma persuaded IPC, a successful publisher of conventional women's magazines, to bring out a magazine for 'the new woman', she described her putative reader as an intelligent housewife, rather well bred, with time to kill and money to spend. *Nova*'s success was in the end due to one man, Dennis Hackett, our Dennis, and it was he as editor, who understood that like every other new woman before, the new woman of the 1960s saw herself as sexy as hell and spiritually at odds with every other magazine in the prosperous IPC group, heavy on knitting patterns and 100 original things to do with Cox's Orange Pippins.

Complaint is a responsibility of growing older. It's up to each generation to keep saying life was better managed when it was young; to complain about the present is a debt of honour we owe our memories. By that token I do not believe that an editor nowadays in London could do what Dennis did then; not since rich cynics started to manipulate the English tendency to think the worst of what they do best – produce high-class newspapers, periodicals, theatre and broadcasting, I mean – has a big publisher, or any other successful company, been persuaded to put the profit principle in jeopardy to sheer bliss. Money, money, over all else, is the philistine's anthem for this age. And yet to this day I sense (I hope) something increasingly unhappy in the

English when they're put to work only for money. An old commandment niggles constantly that it just isn't gentlemanly, it isn't nice, it isn't humane or human, to hold pounds, shillings, pence, or much of anything else, higher than a good time. Even Anglican religious leaders seem to think that we were put on earth as an evolving game, God's hobby, or so it seems from the way they make up the rules as they go along. Only in Britain do actors and stand-up comics emerge in a steady flow from the great classical universities. A Monty Python team out of the Sorbonne, say, is beyond imagining. Loyalty to the antic muse is essentially subversive: nothing can be sacred to men who make fun for a living. The irreverence of English humour is the biggest ostensible difference between the USA and the UK: Americans like to be seen trying to be good and the English prefer to look as if they've given up the attempt. I am one American who finds herself comfortable in London, where a stiff upper lip does not require a straight face. Mind you, native piety must lurk in a few odd corners of my mind, for not long ago, when I heard that a giant ferris-wheel was being proposed as London's salute to the millennium, my first response was: 'Get serious!' In the middle of the night I woke up thinking again: what could be as impudent and minatory, what could be as wholly *Londonish*, as to set a carnival wheel spinning and squealing right across the river from the Houses of Parliament? What is better suited to a citizenry that must struggle always against the forces of pomposity, fundamentalism, self-righteousness and base propriety if they are to survive even into the next thousand years, as Londoners?

A politician is the last thing on earth I could be. Or a chorus girl. I am not a team player. The only team I could ever have served productively would have to have been composed of bad followers, gifted bumblers, enthusiasts, weirdos, and heavy drinkers: a team of amateurs – an English team, in other words. Amateurism is a project of the heart; undertakings the brain turns down out of court, the heart is too stupid to reject: winning a war for instance, the way the bungling Brits did when they held out with elastic bands and colanders against the most precisely trained killing-machine since Julius Caesar. Three days into the new job I had an inkling *Nova* was my kind of team when our beauty editor walked out in a huff and Dennis came through his office door shouting my name.

'You! Write 1000 words on . . . what is this overpriced junk? Moisturisers . . .'

'Dennis, I don't know anything about beauty products.'

'There's bugger all to know about them,' he said. 'Just write about them.'

My beauty copy appeared under the nom de plume, Louise Short: 'The wily and beautiful Cleopatra used river mud and camel dung to repair her ageing skin and keep it soft for Antony . . .' And the immoral of the story is that it also became the single piece of mine to make it into an anthology of contemporary journalism.

We worked out of Tower House in Southampton Street, Covent Garden, which was IPC headquarters in those days. Our office was on an upper floor so there was the risk every morning of sharing the rickety lift with an IPC big-shot. When it happened that I was trapped with one of them, like as not he'd glance my way, clear his throat and begin : 'My wife . . .' Stone me, if she wasn't there with us, an apparition in Wellington boots, twin-set and granny's pearls. '. . . My wife was very upset by your piece in *Nova* last month, the one on sec-sue-ell stereotypes. Found it a bit strong . . .'

'Woof-woof,' said the phantom golden retriever trailing behind the suit's missis. As long as Dennis was editor, each month's issue was like a theatrical first night, and we the players waited anxiously for our reviews to find out if management would let us go on again. Dennis was a practising Catholic and his faith gave his leadership into the darker corners of sex and society an edginess approaching bravado. Homosexuality, urban angst, abortion, infidelity, Russian defectors, California serial killers:

there were no rules to what *Nova* covered and no limits set, least of all because it was ostensibly a magazine for women. Accusations of tastelessness could hardly stand against photographs and layouts of such high style that there wasn't a self-respecting art director from Tokyo to Rio de Janeiro who didn't keep a full set of *Nova*'s in his office. When Dennis had been barely two years in the editor's chair, the men in suits tempted him away from the editorship by giving him a chauffeur-driven car and jumping him on to the board. He still kept an eye on *Nova* but at the same time, the board kept an eye on him. It wasn't long before the magazine entered a pitifull decline, still nice to look at, but shrinking gradually in heat and scope, and finally even in size, until after six or seven years it disappeared over the horizon to the relief of the men in the lift and their families.

There was lots of emotion engaged in the job, but in the beginning and for some time afterwards no backbiting, no competing, no grotesque vanity and none of the crap that makes most office work a misery. We liked each other, and when it comes to business you can't be more amateurish than that. Several of our office romances turned into lasting love. True enough, insults and an occasional inkwell flew between the Fashion Editor and the Art Department, at the same time, however, splendid graphic art emerged from the tantrums, as Dennis knew it would when he found Molly Parkin, heaven alone knows where, and lured her away from painting to become our fashion editor. Because Molly had not done the job before and had never learned what rules could be broken with impunity, she broke them all. Her pages were never less than stunning and often intensely suggestive. Not to say dirty. Molly was a bad, bad girl in those days, God bless her little cotton socks. She often had to be forcibly restrained from stripping off her clothes in public; her language would have knocked a fishwife over at 40 paces; her love-life was baroque, to say the least, and undertaken with inimitable hot brio. When she became exasperated one day while giving me a lift in heavy traffic, I could do nothing but hang on and pray as she took her yellow

Morgan sports-car up over the curb and drove it along the pavement for about 40 yards, as if it were a tricycle. Nobody stopped her either. She was a born mistress of surprise. Oh, how impressed I was the day she arrived at work lisping that she had left her two front teeth in the forearm of number-two lover with whom she'd quarrelled the night before.

'The English aren't supposed to do things like that, Molls,' I said.

She drew herself up to all five foot three.

'Fuck the bloody English,' she said. 'I'm bloody Welsh.'

Thirty years on and Molls is a doting granny. Her two daughters from a first marriage already defunct when we met, are grown up. She was to marry again, a brief and volatile union with the artist Patrick Hughes, the only man of them all, I think, she loved in spite of herself. Molls and I meet every year or so at inescapable parties. The coal-black hair is white. She still has her mobile, mischievous face, no longer geisha-painted in the style of the 60s, helped into age by a shameless televised face-lift. We've come a way, I guess, from the rotgut red we used to knock back in her funny little house in Chelsea. It was painted canary yellow outside and inside was festooned with clothes and hats and jewellery which she hung on the walls as interior decoration. Molly has joined AA, and if I read the signs correctly, she is on the road that leads so many hell-raisers over the hill to be born again as strict Christians.

Americans do laconic, Brits are better at ironic: it's the difference between the actor and the role – between Clint Eastwood and Prince Charles. To be successfully laconic lies mainly in the delivery and it's easy to affect: irony, on the other hand, if it is done without conviction, is just plain silly. Young Brits, or drunk ones, or not very bright ones, never sound sillier than when they try too hard to be ironic. Harri Peccinotti was the only Englishman I've known who gave genuine laconic. Harri was the man who designed *Nova*'s special typeface and its look, as well as already being a world-class photographer back in the 1960s when they were the young princes of media. He is a contradictory and complex sort of guy. His name sings out, the way my own name clunks, in a nation of crisp surnames mainly arriving in long straight lines from places and families, or as homonyms for ordinary things. Coming as I do from a land where names encapsulate histories of exile and miscegenation, I still feel my strangeness sometimes in London's masses of purely Celtic Mcs and Macs and Munros, as well as its Heaths, Thatchers, Majors, Wheelers, Walkers, Whipps and Loaders. When I moved to Soho my widespread wandering moniker was sandwiched between a couple above called the Pickups and one below called the Gatherers. But in spite of his exotic name Harri's antecedents are English, as far as I know, and so are many of his views: he's anti-monarchist, I dare say, and anti-English too, the way many Englishmen are without being pro anything else. Unless I read him wrong, he'd rather have dyed his hair ginger than voted Conservative. But he plays golf. He hates frills and folderol, he used to wear denim overalls to work. He had an eye for models, but as soon as he roped in a dolly-bird, the first thing he did was make her get off her diet and stop wearing make-up. If Harri had a car, I can't recall, but if he had, I'd stake my word it was either a jeep or a Ferrari. You couldn't make him wear a suit; the word 'chic' was not in his vocabulary. But after *Nova* died, he moved to Paris. Every year or so when he's in London he rings me from the pub downstairs. I always recognise his laid-back 'Hello' before he says his name, and we meet for a drink. He never talks much, hardly at all unless I lead him with questions. But we love each other. He's let his beard grow, and he's a big man; he looks like a biblical patriarch. I doubt he'd say that he believes in God, but that's not to say he doesn't.

There were about a dozen of us on the first team, and Dennis was the boss; we knew what we needed to do, so we never had meetings. Too busy. Often as not after work at night we went in small groups or en masse to the local pub; chunks of the magazine were put together in the funky darkness of the Coal Hole. Also of course, we had lunch. It was the lunching decade in London. Everyone had lunch. Decisions were never taken in business between noon and half-past three or four because the decision-makers were all out to lunch; the most imaginative decisions were taken after four, because decision-makers were then back at their desks and inspired by lunch. These London lunches were not like lunches in New York: drink was drunk, for a start, and cigarettes smoked, and because the occasion was primarily social, it was bad form to hustle. Not much ever actually happened then and there at table, but spectacular matches were made, and a lot of unexpected good things, sometimes sexual, were set in motion when compatible minds shared the pleasure of lunch. Strangers sized each other up, probed for strengths and weaknesses, discussed this and that, and ended up becoming each other's first-name contacts on a creative network that served the city well. Back then before time became money and money became the sole reason most people bother to get up in the morning, London would have come to a standstill without its long, long lunches. If ever in history London has had even one tic in common with Los Angeles, which is the city on earth it is most unlike, then it was during that period when restaurants as distinct from *food* became popular on account of the people who turned up there, especially for lunch.

The established restaurants near *Nova* in Covent Garden were popular with big carnivorous men who taxied to them for lunch from the law courts and Whitehall, and who filled the air with 'ho-ho-ho', and 'Quite right, old chap', and the smoke of expensive cigars. When a bright new place called 'The Garden' opened across the street from Tower House, it immediately became a base for *Nova*'s staff as well as for performers from the Opera House and other raffish locals. One lunch-time I was in the downstairs dining-room at the Garden talking to a photographer about life and kicking around a few ideas for stories, when the room went suddenly quiet. Everyone looked up from feeding. Nureyev and

Margot Fonteyn were standing alone at the top of the staircase. She wore a conical hat ringed in fur, like the hat of a Tartar chieftain, and they were both in black. In that moment of serendipity, they made one sharp and singular piece. The Garden is gone, it hardly outlasted *Nova*, there is a shop for camping equipment where it used to be; the dancers have passed on too. But the image of them at the peak of their power stays clear in my memory and I can still see the way they began to move down the steps, in contiguous ripples, like a panther.

On mornings when I was early for work, I used to make a loop of a few blocks from where I got off my bus in the Strand to walk across Covent Garden market. Most cities have had a wholesale food market usually located as the stomach to the heart, below mid-town. Before the fast-food invasion hit Paris, when restaurants there kept strict hours, a traveller unlucky enough to arrive in town after ten could very well go to bed hungry if he didn't know about the all-night brasseries in the market of Les Halles. On many occasions when our talking went on very late in the cafés of the Latin Quarter, Hank and Rho and I joined a few others for sausages there. Talking, talking, we used to walk down the empty streets to the Seine, then over a couple of bridges, and straight into the market. Porters jostled us daylight drudges who were getting under their feet, and the first breath of dawn blew in from the east while night drew itself together behind us like a crouching cat. Les Halles belonged to the butchers in their blood-streaked aprons, they gave the night a coarse, strong, medieval flavour that seeped into the fat sausages we were swilling down with beer.

London on the other hand early on segregated its butchers into Smithfield Market in EC1, where once horses were sold. Meanwhile, Covent Garden's final design was based on an airy conservatory, its smells were green and citric, not rusty and full of gore. Covent Garden's market porters made comments that were sly and positively sylvan compared to what the Rabelaisian meatmen of Paris shouted out to passing women. Pubs in Covent

Garden had a dispensation from licensing hours, and outsiders who turned up there late at night were not looking to stuff their faces, as they were in Paris; they were more rustically in search of ale.

Inner-city wholesale food markets are an anachronism which must all eventually fold, and when they do, they will be converted into tourist attractions. Not that I have anything against tourist attractions, nobody could who has seen the Taj Mahal by moonlight or the Grand Canyon in late October. However, unless tourist attractions are carefully designed they betray the very qualities they are meant to preserve. Les Halles reconstructed has lost the robustness of the market, and the last time I was there it was full of tourists and Parisians trying one way or another to score off each other. Covent Garden, on the other hand, when the market moved on in 1975, was returned to the ideal of a rural fairground by the late, lamented Greater London Council. There are stalls and jugglers, and tables set out in the open air in an ambiance of innocent fun. There is no evidence whatsoever of whores, dubious Turkish baths or gambling dens for which the market square in olden days was a lot more famed than it was for posies and cabbages.

I invited Lillian up to *Nova*'s open-plan office one afternoon to see if she'd like to contribute occasional pieces, and to show off. Jean Penfold, the sub-editor, was the only silent, immobile point in the room; she sat like a statue, a perpetual cigarette wreathed her head in mist, as every last word of copy passed in front of her, and never an error got by. Meanwhile, Molly on the phone was using obscenities that had already once sent the switchboard staff out on strike; a writer was drinking gin at his desk and someone in the art department was dancing with a chair. Lil was horrified: who was taking note of what time employees arrived? How dare a secretary come to work dressed in jeans? Did we all help ourselves to the petty cash, for goodness sake? When she asked about the chain of command I told her Dennis was the boss; the rest of us weren't. She shook her head, and backed away towards the door. Probably, she hadn't minded life all that much in jail.

Lil and her mother had moved again and were living in a large basement flat in west London. Lil had an eye for good-looking men, superfluous though it was, and at one of the gay clubs she went to, she met a tall dark Englishman whose very rich old ga-ga American lover had recently been kidnapped by kin and spirited home to Indiana. Chris needed a place to live, and Lil offered him a room in exchange for general housekeeping and for keeping an eye on Angelica who was becoming more and more forgetful. The first time I saw Chris, he was cleaning the top of the kitchen cupboard. 'Honestly,' he said looking down from his step-ladder, 'you women are such slobs.' Chris cleaned, cooked, and once in a while after the more extravagant quarrels between Lil and Angelica, he swept up the broken glass, tut-tutting. Every evening when Lil came home from work she found a whisky and her slippers waiting. Oberon bit Chris once, it was hardly more than a love nip. Chris had the nerve to put Lil on a diet, and she used to show me proudly the big tucks he had to take in the waistbands of her skirts. His rule on her home-life was fussy and absolute; and she loved complaining to me about it. In that period as in no other during all the years I was to know Lil, she seemed almost contented.

Meanwhile, Rhoda had become friendly with an English poet and his wife who lived in Norfolk; she used to visit them every week or so, and then come on to me for a few days in London before going back to Paris. Hank had finally moved out of their flat to live with a Dutch girlfriend in Amsterdam. Rhoda's mockery of his infidelity seemed enviable to one like me who was easily hurt in love. She was planning to leave Paris and 'give London a try', she said, as if the city were up for her employ. Each time she passed through, she left behind clothes and books at my place in Chelsea. Her paintings began to accumulate in my hall, too. I leaned them against the wall on the floor and put a few of them up whenever she was due to visit. They were of parrots in cages hanging over the heads of seated male figures, or men in chairs dwarfed by monstrous swiss-cheese plants. I wondered if all the figures were faceless because Rhoda could not draw faces; later I decided it was because she could not see any but her own.

9

Notting Hill Gate

'America . . .' sighed Dennis's secretary when I told her where I was going to be for the next fortnight.

America: the very sounds lend themselves to sighing.

America: it isn't something boys want to yell when they're rolling around in the mud or breaking each other's noses, not like: Ing-lund! Ing-lund!

'Am-aiaiairica. The United States of Am-aiaiairica!' she sighed. 'What wouldn't I give . . .?'

The USA was a distant and mysterious destination for Europeans in the late 1960s, more distant still and mysterious for me. For me, a return to America was a journey in time as well as space, and time-travel, especially when it turns the clock back, is more dangerous and disorientating in every way than straight-forward travel in space. When I'd last seen my native country, Kennedy Airport on Long Island was called Idlewild; the youngest president in the history of the nation had barely been inaugurated, and there were a few years in hand before the crack of a rifle in Dallas was going to shake America out of its beauty sleep. The year I sailed away, the average high-school senior would have said Vietnam was part of the Philippines, wasn't it? Horn and Hardart had not long before stopped making the best creamed spinach in living memory; a subway token was a dime. In those days, we ordinary folks couldn't afford the luxury of air travel, we had to cross the Atlantic by boat. Since then of course, as a London-based journalist, I had flown from propeller to jet all over Europe. But I had been out of my homeland for seven years, and until my plane touched down at Kennedy Airport I had not yet set foot in an American airport.

'Welcome back, Irma,' said the US immigration official from behind his high desk. Cool as St Peter, he leaved through his big black book in which were noted sins to confound non-desirable aliens.

'You know, Irma,' he said, fixing me on twin beams of virtue as he handed back my passport, 'it's about time you came home.'

I passed through big doors into a steamy blast of hot New York fug that was louder than a whole summer of noise in London, and heavy with forgotten ordinary smells: yellow mustard, burnt sugar, melting tar and the sweat of over-fed people. Giants pushed past me for taxis and yelled to each other over my head.

Since then, for the past twenty years and more I have flown back to America two or three times most years, and at least one of the annual journeys is to New York. I don't really need to go to New York, for most of the year my mother is where my brother lives in California, and I have very few friends in Manhattan. It isn't duty that draws me there, or a social life. Nor is it shopping, even though New Yorkers are truly gifted in that department, shopping more shrewdly than Londoners, more adventurously than Parisians or Angelenos, and altogether more diligently than any other city-people on earth.

Certainly I do not go for theatre to New York: who would go for the theatre to any city where it is customary to interrupt proceedings and applaud the entrance of each leading actor on stage? Harrumph! When I go to New York, I don't do much at all, only see a friend or two. I order a chicken-salad platter at any cheap luncheonette on Sixth Avenue to admire again the way the scoops – pink (chicken), green (slaw), white (potato) salad – are always plunked precisely on tomato slices that are set like wagon-wheels in a froth of chopped lettuce. There must be a school somewhere in the city with courses in chicken-salad platters. Then I walk up and down town, across and over, hour after hour, waiting for my thrill; I never know on what street it will overtake me, morning or afternoon, sometimes in the rain, and only when I'm alone. I make my annual pilgrimage to New York, and will continue to do so as long as I am able, for that one charged moment that only Manhattan can deliver when suddenly everything is as good as new, for a flash the air sparkles again with genuine gold-dust, and the stage-struck child I used to be jumps up on tiptoe to applaud the entrance of a star. My guess is that all kids remain forever starry-eyed about the first great city they see, even after they have left it for another.

New York is a neurotic mother, scolding and sentimental, beloved yet impossible to live with, suffocating, hypochondriacal, and forever moving the furniture. Of my four former addresses, only the brownstone on West 112th Street is still standing. It's not just the changing architecture that throws memory out of kilter, the city's mood-swings are equally disconcerting. On my first trip back after seven years, everyone was in a mist of happiness; even the taxi driver who took me mid-town from the airport was good-humoured and eager to please. Barely a year later, back again, weather as good, no recent disasters, economy not bad, mayor is a Democrat, and not only does my first taxi driver curse me out when he can't make change for ten dollars, every native in sight is low and snarling, and not somebody to meet on a dark street.

'Don't take it poisonal, lady,' the taxi driver said in surly apology as he roared off, leaving me short-changed in front of the Port Authority.

Violence rumbles and gathers and organises in the cities of Europe, and finally explodes at a selected location or sometimes in choreographed riots; in India and Far Eastern cities, it surges and rolls mindlessly in a ground-swell, like a natural disaster. But New York's violence can occur anywhere at any time, erupting out of accidental collisions of interest on the crowded pavements.

It's the only city I know outside a war zone in which a pedestrian can bump into a police chase on foot, and a little later see a well-dressed man struggling against arrest in the packed aisles of a department store. Unique pathologies afflict New Yorkers too, and obsess them, though rarely for more than a year at a time. Come back a year later and ask politely after cholesterol levels or hypoglycaemia, Lyme Disease, Stress Related Syndrome or whatever worried New York friends last time, and they'll describe the symptoms of a brand new threat to their health. When scientists started to warn us publicly about global pollution, I happened to be in New York and every local I talked to about the hole in the ozone layer was sure he was sitting directly under it.

'Eat broccoli,' my Manhattan hostess said, and she brought out a platter of the stuff, half-raw. 'Eat broccoli, and live forever.'

All Americans believe in their secret hearts that death is the result of bad advice or carelessness, and New Yorkers have the added paranoid zest of being more heavily than anyone else outside Washington DC into conspiracy theories. If there were really life after death, believe me, a New Yorker would have made it back by this time to bring a suit against his bum of a doctor.

College friends had long ago left Manhattan to raise their families in less congested places, or they were Professing Modern Poetry on western campuses. For many years the single person I saw or stayed with in New York was someone I met, not there, but in Tunisia in the early 1960s. By chance she and I had chosen the same cheap boarding-house in Houmt Soukh on the Island of Djerba. If I were making a film of the Old Testament, I'd cast Irene as a deep-breasted, green-eyed Esther eating cakes under the gallows where Haman's sons were hanging. At first I thought she must be a member of the Peace Corps, so impassioned and promiscuous was her enthusiasm for every last thing in the Third World, right down to the translucent scorpion which haunted our bathroom. It turned out she was an illustrator for animated films, a fiddling job for so big and impatient a woman, and she also illustrated children's books, though she had no great love for children. When I told Irene how long I'd been living in London she looked pained, the way immigration officers at LAX and Kennedy sometimes do when confronted by someone lucky enough to be born American, who actually chooses to live abroad. Every city is a secret society, and London is more exclusive than most. Ancient and insular formalities are attached to its trades and pastimes, each street name and little alley is part of a code of such subtlety and complexity that it is a life's work to learn it, and Londoners, I'm afraid, must be to the manner born. On the other hand, it's easy to become a bonafide New Yorker. In fact, New Yorkers are proud of their city and typical of it are those who grew up somewhere else. Irene was a Russian-born Jew whose family had been chased all over Europe, one jump ahead of the Nazis. When they finally arrived in the USA she was still only a kid, young enough to start again without all the bitter wounds of older refugees. Irene was as devoted to New York, and to the United States, as a shipwrecked passenger to a lifeboat. At the same time, her taste in literature and music was romantic and erudite, she spoke five languages fluently and her sensuality and boiling passions sometimes made her cruel: all in all, her soul was as Russian as it could be.

Anywhere Irene called home became in no time a welter of chipped relics, curios, souvenirs, and over-filled ashtrays, wayward house-plants racing for light, crumpled papers, bent forks, gnawed crusts, gristle, bones, empty tins, stained books, broken goblets and velvet rags. She liked to cook big, sloppy meals; she ate a lot and smoked continuously. I've known some slobs in my time, never one as exuberant as she. On my first trip back to New York, and for many subsequent trips, I used to stay with her in her one-bedroom flat over a fur store on West 57th Street; after the building was torn down, she moved into a bigger apartment uptown on the West Side. In her kitchens, the sink was eternally full of greasy dishes in cold water flecked with cigarette stubs and drowned cockroaches. Her person was clean and smelled good, but the extreme neglect of hygiene and order in her territory could be counted as self-abuse.

Irene's father had been a film-director in Europe; he made a few second-features in America too, and his name pops up late at night on old movie channels. Bald as a narrow squeak, with eyes that held defeat and a dark amusement, he was distantly flirtatious. Irene adored him and blamed her mother's selfishness for his relatively youthful death which happened not long after I met him. Her mother lived on the upper East Side in an apartment of some style which Irene visited only under duress. I'd been coached to say Irene was out whenever I answered the phone and it was her mother on the line.

'Tell Iron,' her mother said on her tenth attempt to get through one day, 'dot I am dyink . . .'

She let the receiver drop and must have given it a hard push to make it thud ominously against the wall.

'She'll never die,' Irene said when I told her, and went in search of her big scrofulous pink-eyed cat, 'Pickles', who was usually to be found lurking under the kitchen sink, chewing on a gruesome tidbit. She dragged him out, threw him in the air, then kneaded him roughly into the carpet with her strong inky hands while he purred. Irene alone could touch the beast and expect to come away unventilated. 'Pickles' was every bit as fierce as Lillian's dog. It's as well the animals never met. Irene didn't like London very much, its glamour was too low key for her taste, and she mistook English restraint for failure of emotions.

'Irene,' I pleaded with her, 'who do you imagine needs to restrain emotions if not those who feel them dangerously, to the core?'

English courtesy sounded to her like sarcasm, and her Russian pride was constantly on guard for insults in London. Sensitive polyglot though she was, she could not bring herself to understand the American language used in any other way or spoken in an accent other than that of the country she'd come to as a homeless child. Because a kind of English accent is put on by pretentious Americans, my otherwise worldly friend Irene, like some other Americans I've known, took the English accent as an affectation among the English too, and a sign of fakery.

'*Do* come and see us before you go back to the States,' a local friend said when I introduced them, and Irene glowered, having perversely heard the '*Do*' as '*Don't*'.

Nip back to New York after a year away and everything will have changed from its fad food to its latest mortal fear; everyone is bursting with new opinions, a new celebrity is flavour of the month. On the other hand, I've left London and then returned from a war in Vietnam, from learning how to Scuba dive in Barbados, from the stark red outback of Australia, from Moscow under snow, India, Mexico, from a year's meandering around the world, from half a year on Greyhound buses through the American hinterland, from practically everything, practically everywhere, and pausing only to drop my unpacked bags on the living-room floor, I've raced out into the good old left-handed streets, starving for news, hungering to share my stories, and every friend I've greeted wildly has looked at me with surprise and said: 'You back already?' London is in the zone of elephants and whales and other big, clever, slow-moving animals. My first day home in London from every odyssey abroad and the newsagent on Shaftesbury Avenue, where for ten years I've bought my daily papers, does not fail to look up from counting out my change to ask: 'Been away, then?'

London has seen the bottom of grief in its time and learned to husband emotions. Somewhere along the line of its long history it came to the end of its capacity for hysteria. Tell a Londoner his city is directly under a hole in the ozone layer, he won't tear his hair or go on a weird diet: he'll say something like. 'Zatso? Meet me down the Coach and Horses, we'll see what we can do to plug it up.' Compared to other capitals, the pace of London life is slow, much slower than Londoners themselves imagine as they cope with the irritations of life in any big city, exacerbated when the weather is bad, or when the streets are wall to wall with

Manchester United supporters down for a match at Wembley. Even in the late 1960s while London was swinging to beat the band, it showed a calm surface next to Paris where the barricades were going up again. While Chelsea and Westminster fussed about the mini-skirt and quibbled over laws of decency, Chicago was quelling demonstrations with a brutality that set some kind of precedent for the shooting by the National Guard a couple of years later of four students at Kent State University. The kids were protesting against the war in Vietnam which, it turned out, was not part of the Philippines after all. Meanwhile every shiny little creature in the swim in London was loopy for drugs and sex; and *Nova* was a local celebrity pulling those of us who worked on it in its wake. We were having a ball. I barely noticed the passing of my early thirties except that peaks were higher than ever, and therefore the valleys had to be lower.

For the young and those who passed as young, the whole city was an open-house for partying. Celebrities from all over the world passed through to clock the action, and lots of them left later visibly out of sorts because nobody had paid attention to them. Londoners have a resistance to famous people, traffic doesn't stop for them, and even the kids hardly ever carry on so madly over pop stars that they require police control. Movie stars are often to be seen sitting in West End clubs, alone. Alone. Or even sometimes just standing around the streets, looking puzzled and a little scared. Native reserve and courtesy are only part of the explanation. The main reason Londoners are slow to adulate is that they believe that anyone who is world-famous cannot be all that good at what he does. It is another anarchical London street view with which I wholeheartedly concur: being famous absorbs valuable time and ambition, and the famed one is very soon parted from what he's famous for.

Journalists come cap in hand to an interviewee, they are beggars of the moment, and that's probably why editors so often put women to work interviewing famous men, especially, and why so often we take vengeance for our humiliation by turning in pieces of pure vitriol. During my time on *Nova* I profiled literally tons of international celebrities. Out of all the famous people I interviewed and nearly met, there would not have been even one I would have liked to know better except that among my interviewees were John Huston, Paul Scofield and John Lennon. When celebrities turned up at parties or at the next table, which they did all the time on the easy-going London scene, they were short. Who lived in Earl's Court on Trebovir Road? William Burroughs lived there for a while, I've been told, but I never even nearly met him. Whoever it was, gave a party late in the 1960s. There were the usual pop stars and famous models, and Douglas was there, too. We hadn't met for several years, and it took a moment for memory to fit itself to his face. First his eyes came back, oh sure, of course. Like words in an easy crossword puzzle, one by one other features fell into place. We had nothing much to say to each other, a few awkward words and vague assurances that we must get together while he was in London. The young girl he had been dancing with, someone told me later, was the daughter of his first marriage; the young girl with whom he soon left the party was his latest wife. I watched him dance and saw him leave with an achy resignation that was the oldest feeling I'd ever felt.

A love affair with a colleague was turning out to be more exclusive and enduring than it should have been. He was one of those northerners who had married a childhood sweetheart early on and then moved south to make good in the big city. Phenomenal energy buzzed around him and pushed everything in front of it, including my reservations about affairs with married men. The guy was a rider rough-shod, I have to say, more industrious, ambitious and inclined to power than my usual lovers who on the whole have been London grasshoppers. The truth is, I was not crazy about my married lover, nor was he about me. But Paris and New York were his dream-sites while he was growing up, and their glamour had rubbed off on me, the way it does on the mistresses of famous men. We could hardly dignify ourselves as the storm-tossed victims of passion; our affair was tawdry and self-indulgent, which made it even harder on his wife when she found out. Careless though the times were, I was too careless. The move I made from Chelsea to Notting Hill Gate wasn't particularly joyous or significant: it was my come-uppance.

Notting Hill Gate has some of the louche charm of a frontier town. It is a kind of outpost where travellers on the long trek to London's westernmost edge will find their last arty cinema, their last antiquarian bookstore; their last five-star hotel is down the road, and when I moved into the area, 'The Gate' still offered them their last chance to stock up at a decent delicatessen before embarking on rough travel into the hinterlands of North Hammersmith, Acton and Ealing. Hippie squats and encampments used to be scattered north of the Portobello Road where my son tells me people go now for reggae, drugs and soul food. Up-market addresses and some of the grandest houses in central London are tucked away beyond the range of tourists who throng out of the Underground for the antique market on Saturday morning. Since 1966 the Notting Hill Carnival, mounted annually by London's West Indian community, has put haughty noses out of joint locally when it percolates throughout 'The Gate' and its environs like the invasion of a dancing nation. My married lover was friendly with an architect and his wife who wanted to let their upstairs flat in one of the prettiest of the crescents that radiated off Ladbroke Grove, near Notting Hill Gate. Chelsea was swinging from twee to more twee and was starting to get on my nerves. I liked the idea of having a nearby launderette again, and a butcher, and no shoe-stores, and a newsagent who didn't sell tee-shirts on the side. A big bright flat in a residential area was tempting, the rent was a mere three pounds more per week than I was paying, I would be the only tenant in the building, and I had not accumulated so much that moving was a major undertaking.

I was still grabbed by an American small-town notion of 'best friendship' between two girls, with all the dated rules of conduct it entailed: daily phone calls in which we took it in turns to talk to ourselves out loud, letters when we were not in the same city, postcards from long-distance trips. Best friends hold each other's secrets, too, but I've never had many secrets, and Rhoda's secrets were vital to her very being, so to share them was too dangerous to risk. The symbolic lending of clothes between best friends was not on either: she let me know that she could not afford the clothes she wanted, and when she wanted something of mine, I gave it to her. Irene was a more sympathetic companion, and had she lived nearer, we probably would have been in each other's pockets for a while, as best friends are. From the beginning, Rhoda and I had merely been imitating the rituals, best friends only for convenience driven together among strangers by the fact of being two Americans abroad, and remaining friends later out of habit. At the time of course I simply called Rhoda my best friend and took it as read. She stayed in my London flat while I was in New York, and there was no question that she would take it over when I moved to Notting Hill.

'You'll have to be vetted by the Colonel of Cadogan Square.'

'No problem,' she said. 'Lend me your black suit.'

Nova's new editor took beauty a lot more seriously than Dennis had. A few months after Rhoda moved into my Chelsea flat, I fixed for her to have the skin of her pock-marked face planed in exchange for a piece and photographs for *Nova*'s beauty pages. After each sand-papering session Rhoda had to hole up while her face healed under an encasement of bloody gauze, and I used to deliver her groceries to what a little while before had been my own place. Except for Rhoda's paintings on all the walls, nothing had changed – same curtains, same beat up sofa, she had not replaced any of the pretty objects I'd collected and taken with me – the poor little flat was looking bleak and I was perplexed, as I would have been by any woman's failure to cherish her first home on her own. My old television was still in its corner after a month in spite of arrangements for it to be picked up so my deposit could be reimbursed. Television sets were expensive relative to the average salary, they regularly needed repair and they rapidly became obsolete, so it was common practice in London to hire a set instead of buying one.

'I guess I was asleep when they came to get it,' Rhoda said. 'Don't worry. I'll take care of it as soon as I feel better.'

The deposit was twenty pounds, as I recall, a considerable sum then, which at the sort of interest banks have charged over these past 26 or so years comes to something like 5000 quid Rho would owe me now.

Traditionally, when a man finds his girlfriend a flat, it's to set up a ménage. But in the event, after I was installed at 'The Gate', the married man and I rarely met again unless it was at work or by chance. For all my soul's yearning, right to the end I could not stay in love with a man who threatened to take me away from the mix of tedium and discipline and frustrated desire that is a woman's independence.

10

Lansdowne Crescent

Photographers and hair-dressers were London's darlings at the end of the 1960s and well into the 70s. Painters, poets and many journalists mixed with the middle-aged leftovers of London's 1950s bohemia who continued to drink themselves traditionally stuporous in Soho, an alcoholic old guard who despised the parties of pot-smoking acid-dropping youngsters and dis-approved of soft drugs as righteously as church-fête matrons. Pop stars in groups of four or five were a phenomenon born of the time and moving smartly to the top of the social scene. Coming up fast on the outside was a group of London-based therapists, the anti-analysts they called themselves, whose main thrust (in a nutshell) was that the mad, and the mad alone, made sense. A number of the anti-shrink shrinks were Irishmen, ever to be found around poetic madness, and quite a few of the rest were Americans verging on expatriation, motivated by politics and who knows what permutations of the Oedipus complex? Popular hallucinogenic drugs of the time abetted their crusade for all us victims of sanity to commune with the lunatic within. Snappers, troubadours, crimpers and the occasional anti-shrink shrink: a party in London wasn't off the ground until one or two of them had arrived in pixie-boots with a pocketful of dope.

Photographers were given star treatment and high fees that irritated the rest of us jobbing hacks, especially when we were sent together on assignment abroad where they showed a regal incapacity to grasp local currencies and funny foreign ways. Nevertheless, photographers were by and large a disarmingly boyish lot, comparable to racing-car drivers, charmers of their special world: half man, half machine. As for the pop stars, electronic gizmos weren't up to much yet so the success of a pop group was due as often to their packaging and their lyrics as it was to musicianship, which many barely had. Although they affected the manners of football hooligans and the accents of yobs, in those affectedly classless days they sometimes turned out to be smarter and a lot better educated than they looked. Emergent pop stars aimed straight for the high life: they made all the best parties, stayed at all the best hotels, travelled first-class, were seen around town with models and particularly enjoyed the company of lords. In London back then lords were thick on the ground, at pubs and trattorias, at parties and concerts, shopping in Carnaby Street. Peers were often photographed with pop stars, and as the 60s passed into the 1970s it became increasingly hard to tell which was in the other's entourage. As for the anti-shrink shrinks, they were the darlings of Hampstead and similar traditionally liberal enclaves of north-west London where they held court rather than parties; they also appeared more often in print than in public.

When it comes to temporal designs and fashion, Britain is a man's country, supreme only in haberdashery. London has had great tailors and shirtmakers, hatmakers, bootmakers, gunsmiths and saddlers; no London dressmaker has ever been a patch on Balenciaga or Givenchy or Chanel, no stunning perfume has come out of an English lab, and to this day the sexiest silk underwear is imported. In general, the chief gift of these islands was not plastic or even visual; in spite of a few sculptors of note, and a handful of painters, Britain's great flowering was literary. Precisely why London came to contain the best hairdressers for women in the world is a cunning little piece to fit into the puzzle, and so is how hairdressers in the 1960s managed to acquire cachet in society. Granted they were excellent at what they did, but then so were accountants and estate agents, and nobody expected to sit next to them at lordly dinner-tables, not for another ten years or so. The way I see it, when bobs and perms brought coiffure out of the closet, the hairdresser became a sort of technician, hardly more than an animated buzz in the machinery, until the 1960s when the London fashion scene became coiffure-based. Suddenly, hair was 'in', and all sorts of vaguely trendy, lazy young Englishmen with previously small prospects saw an easy way to get ahead, and incidentally too, to get their hands on lots and lots of females who would otherwise be out of their league. Fewer male hairdressers than jokes and TV farce would have us think are gay; a far larger proportion of them than, say, dress designers, turn out to be heterosexual and very randy too, in a persistent, indolent, really quite English way. Presentable young men of the 1960s wanting a shot at the big-time could do a lot worse than learn how to copy styles in hair, a knack like ice-sculpting I imagine, while simultaneously reacting to the confessional chit-chat of the head in their hands. When a woman stood up from her hairdresser's chair and smiled at herself, this way and that, reflected back from the mirror was a glow of satisfaction that was practically post-coital. For as long as her hair stayed in style – a day or two, not more than a week – strange men turned towards her heat. She wouldn't dream of going to an important rendezvous unless she'd first been to her hairdresser for a treatment. Naturally, in the egalitarian spirit of 1960s London, women invited crimpers to their parties. And to Barbados. And went to bed with them, if the dear boys were so inclined. A few vain and insecure clients married their hairdressers, hoping that way never to lose the man in whose hands rested their cosmetic satisfaction. Hairdressing became a libertine's charter, enhanced by the logistics of the procedure: what Don Juan wouldn't do his best work when spared any need to look at the woman he is handling, eye to eye? And no man in the world could take more enthusiastically to this position than an Englishman, whose ego is by nature more flighty than forward.

'Why are London hairdressers the best in the world?' I asked

Donald after I'd begun having my own hair dressed regularly.

'Nothing suits an Englishman better,' he replied, 'than to tender service from behind.'

Not long after I moved to Notting Hill Gate, the time came at last to have my hair cut. I was a distaff Samson, my hair had never before been cut professionally; it was long enough to wrap around my throat several times and use as a scarf when the weather was blustery or, less functionally, I could sit on it. Long hair had been freedom: from hairdresser, from convention, and from fashion. It had also made travelling easier than a fussy hairstyle. A few twists, a few pins and it took care of itself until the pins came out and the dark tumble turned into an erotic signal that was flagrant and at the same time curiously virginal, like a lace fan, or a waft of jasmine But a long-haired woman if she's smart, crops the mop before she's afraid she'd be lost without it, long before straggling grey turns the thoughts of men from nymph to earth-mother, or witch. Being new at the crimping business, and fearful of making a fool of myself – how much did one tip? who did one tip? was the coffee free? – I didn't dare go to any of the crimpers with weird names who were famous around London, or even to one of the Johns or Alans or Terrys who was prefaced with 'Mister', a title of respect also applied to master tattooists, I've been told. Molly Parkin had recently had her own hair dyed green, and she was au fait with the crimping scene. Molls put me on to a married couple called Evansky who ran a salon in Duke Street that was respected without being trendy. Assisted by her husband, Rose snipped away very slowly, stopping every inch or so in case I'd changed my mind. Like most of humankind under 50 I fancied myself to be an 'either/or individual' who only went for the ardent extremes. But the Evansky team flatly refused to cut shorter than shoulder-length: 'Not your first time,' Rose said. They straightened wayward kinks under a dryer according to the fashion of the time, then sprayed me with some sort of stinking glaze, and by the time I stood up from the chair I was no longer the very image of a bohemian's French peasant, or a Barnard college swat. When I left Evansky's, I'd been transformed hair-wise into a London dolly-bird, and strands of myself begun thousands of miles away in another country were being swept out by a junior into the gutter of Mayfair.

My flat in Lansdowne Crescent was as far up the property ladder in London as I was destined to lay my head, at least, in my own bed. It represents the peak of the area's classical style, the most beautiful of the streets that branch off the central trunk of Ladbroke Grove which afterwards runs north into shabbiness and neglect. I had a living-room and a bedroom on the top floor, and above it a converted loft made just the kind of study any writer needs: it was impossible for anyone over four feet tall to stray more than a foot from the desk without being smacked on the head by the steep slopes of the ceiling. Bedroom and oak-panelled bathroom looked out on a private communal garden completely enclosed between the backs of the houses in our crescent and those of the next crescent over. The cooing of a family of collared doves was the first sound I heard most summer mornings when I woke up. My living-room windows gave out on to a view of spanking white houses mirroring ours on the opposite side of the quiet street. Many years later my son was unusually impressed to learn that his mum used to live next door to the house where Jimi Hendrix died and from her window she had seen the ambulance that came for him. None of the neighbours was as nosy as neighbours were in New York, nor were any of them as hostile as my Parisian neighbours used to be, and my landlords, with whom I shared an entry hall, were all but invisible. The Crescent was set in London aspic, silent and elegant and thick, and so properly made that it always came as a small surprise to find Notting Hill Gate jumping around a few blocks away, and an Underground that had me in the West End within fifteen minutes. In the quiet early hours, when I paused at the steps in front of our house to put out my rubbish, having packed it neatly for collection, it seemed all other human life must have been wiped out the night before. Had I dreamed London? Had I been kidnapped by aliens and taken in my sleep to an empty capital? Then a Mini or BMW parked along the Crescent pulled away from the curb, the man or woman at the wheel indisputably human, though barely visible behind tinted glass, leaving me on a conventional middle-class London street.

Hans Werner Henze, the German composer whom I had interviewed in Italy, came over for tea when he was visiting London, and he left behind two handsome young protégés who needed a place to stay for a while. One of them was Dani Cohn-Bendit who I hear is a plump green politico in Germany these days. At the time 'Dani the Red' was admired everywhere in the world where young people were planning revolution; he was not all that well known in London. The other boy was the German firebrand, Rudi Dutschke. Rudi was intelligent and fierce, and apparently he meant every word he said for he did not make old bones. My goodness, could those two boys talk! with the volume of Paris in the old days, though what they had to say was more cynical than our arty palaver, and they were much more apprised of evil than café philosophers at the end of the 50s and into the early 60s. While the boys talked and talked, and ate, smoked, drank and talked, and slept in my upstairs study, men in raincoats watched the house from the front seats of a series of cars that would have looked ordinary enough except they had too many aerials. The presence of fuzz (yclept) didn't suit Lansdowne Crescent, especially when they got out to stretch their legs and marched around like extras on the set of *Oliver*. From my window I watched one of them grind a cigarette out on his gloved hand, rather than drop it on the pavement. Policemen were a lot more ill at ease in the Crescent than the revolutionaries who seemed perfectly at home and were in no great hurry to leave.

Any land where a multiplicity of choices is considered freedom, will need a lot of adjectives, and for Americans the cost of an object becomes one of its adjectives, defining it, while attesting to the ambitions of its owner. When an American talks about his 'twenty-thousand dollar car' or his 'ten-million dollar Degas', he's said a mouthful. In New York however, the consumer's pride thrives as close as it can get to the wholesale price, and when New Yorkers boast it's usually about paying less for their best things than you have paid for yours. My father was in this way a true New Yorker: whatever it was you had or wanted, he'd got it or knew where to get it cheaper. On the lower East Side in New York where he was born at the turn of the century, poverty was real and cruel and grinding, and poverty remained one of several habitual dreads that hung around his head like bad dreams from the night before. Long after my father had turned himself into a prosperous man, we lived homoeopathically in an imitation of poverty, scaring it off with a taste of its own medicine. Remembering poverty my father dreaded extravagance, and so he used to scour second-hand shops and off-beat auctions, sometimes for suitcases people left behind when they did a bunk on a hotel bill, or jumped out of a window. I tagged along and inherited his passion for rummaging. While he ran his thumb along used tools and appliances to test for any life left in them, I sifted through pirates' chests that spilled out torn and faded handbags, wallets, left-footed shoes, empty boxes shaped like hearts that still smelled faintly of chocolate and were trimmed with lace, broken toys of children long ago grown up – dead? – snapshots of strangers and groups of strange friends, old books and costume jewellery. I was about eight years old the first time an object leapt into my hand, proclaiming magic. It was a silver brooch in the shape of a fish, gleaming and trembling, set with a piece of yellow glass. I found it in a box of old clothes at the Goodwill Store and I bought it for ten cents. I still have it: my first hunting trophy. There were going to be plenty of bright, strange objects coming my way later, some I acquired and others I couldn't really afford at the time: a beaded snake in Istanbul, a ring of ancient keys in Aix-en-Provence, a jailbird's painting of his last courtroom on a stall in an east London market. And I can see every brush-stroke on the small triptych showing Christ entering Jerusalem. I rooted it out of a pile of old wood in Greece and wanted it so much it hurt, but I hadn't fifteen dollars to spare. Rhoda took it out of my hand: 'Get it for me,' she told Hank.

Until I settled down in London my magpie urge had been frustrated by penury and I could kid myself that it was under control. But I hadn't counted on making my home in a city where rooting around junk shops is a local sport. New York is for a bargain, Paris is for great labels, and London is where to go to collect the bits that are constantly dropping off social history: shagreen cigarette cases, first editions about the Second World War, magnifying glasses with scrimshaw handles, ink-wells that romantic poets dipped into, black telephones with dials, scales and weighing machines, art nouveau, art deco, lace-up shoes and shoe-trees, everything and anything the past has left behind or thrown away. There's hardly a London high street without at least as many junk shops as pubs, and I have yet to meet a Londoner who does not hunt through the detritus of time in an old, old city for whatever is his or her kind of treasure.

A few blocks from Lansdowne Crescent was the Portobello Road that every Saturday turned into what is now known widely as an antique market; back then it was a glorified junk market. Not a Saturday went by without a trundle there in search of some useless thing that sang to me. Tony, my son's father-to-be, was a painter with a keen eye who shared my addiction to flea markets and junk shops. Rummaging is a loner's pastime, however, and we soon made it a rule to browse separately; his way was as specific as my father's had been though not as pragmatic. He was highly critical in an amused, scoffing painterly way, and much less impulsive than I. We used to travel to street markets further afield and less well known than the Portobello. Very early most Fridays, in the London dawn that is moist with sweet possibilities, we used to pile into his beat-up yellow car and head south of the river to the Bermondsey Market, where trading began by torchlight. Thanks to an ancient charter, stolen goods could be bought and sold with impunity at the Bermondsey. Local police constables used to advise householders who had been recently burgled to scout the Bermondsey and Petticoat Lane markets where they'd have a chance to buy their bric-à-brac back at knock-down prices. And that, by the by, was about as mean as it got back then in the residential streets and crescents of W11.

London life had started to be comfortable. I could hear massive doors swinging slowly closed to lock me in for keeps if I hung around much longer, and wanderlust was nipping at my heels. One winter day near the end of 1969, Molly Parkin and I were having lunch at a restaurant in Park Lane; I don't remember what brought us to such an unlikely part of London. 'Poncey', Molls called the stretch of hotels that were separated by a river of traffic from Hyde Park, and by five-star insulation from the reality of a city where even in the 60s central heating was not par for the course and ice-cubes were a special request. Molls was wearing a green satin turban with a purple trouser suit, her bracelets keeping up a background timpani to the penetrating Welsh resonances of her words. A group of American women at the next table seemed undecided whether Molly was local colour or something more dangerous, possibly contagious.

We were into our second carafe of red wine. I'd been bemoaning a lack of adventure in my life. Even though I was regularly sent abroad for interviews and general features the travel was too clean, too safe and comfortable, too much like staying at home.

'Did I expatriate myself just to become part of the English establishment?' I cried. Molls echoed: 'Establishment cunts!'

'Why must anyone denigrate a person's sex organs?' asked the largest of the Americans, rhetorically and loud; they turned their backs and did not look our way again.

Before the carafe was finished I'd moved into world-ranging complaints, until, finally exasperated, Molly said as I was coming on so strong against the American presence in Vietnam, then what was I waiting for? A gold-edged invitation? Why didn't I just go on over there and put the boyos right? The bill arrived.

'Ponces,' Molly said, peeling off fivers, 'cunts.'

Arm in arm we sauntered to the offices of Qantas Airways not far away, and she waited in the lobby of the Ritz Hotel while I went and collared a young Australian press officer. He understood why I wanted to go sort out Vietnam; he was worried sick about it too.

'But we don't fly to Saigon . . .'

'Singapore then? I'll make my own way from there.'

'No probs . . .'

And thus, three months later on a rainy February morning, there was my heart racing ahead of me again to unknown places as I set out alone from Heathrow with a first-class ticket around the world *gratis* from Qantas Airways. I'd spent the months between setting up freelance work and putting together expense money. It really was as easy as that. Things used to be easy in those days, for some of us anyhow. A year later when I'd come home from my travels Molly told me that the sympathetic Aussie who had given me my ticket suffered a serious nervous breakdown soon afterwards, and they'd shipped him back to Perth. Poor chap.

I took the world by leaps and bounds, faster than I'd dreamed of doing it when I was a child, breathlessly, watchfully, and alone. From waking up in the genteel stillness of Lansdowne Crescent, within a few hours I found myself curling up to sleep in a small unventilated room on the sub-continent of India. And no time later, there was I sprawled on the steps of a disused temple overgrown with dry grasses, waiting for a bus that was supposed to pass there on its way to Bangalore. The air was full of strange small noises and a smell like grated nutmeg. Feeling absolutely all there and in my skin, I leaned back against the warm stone. Suddenly from the tan sweep of land rose a thousand parakeets, they filled the sky with a strident emerald rush. I had never been as happy; I knew I had never been happier. My route was east to Madras, mostly on trains or buses. You could say I was working my way around the world, in relatively cushy fashion. I interviewed Arthur C. Clarke in Sri Lanka for *Nova,* and Mrs Bandaranaike for the *Observer,* I think; in Bombay I filed a piece on the movie industry for the Qantas in-flight magazine, and a Scottish newspaper supplement asked me to interview a heart-stoppingly handsome actor who met me in his penthouse overlooking the seething port. In the air, on board Qantas, life was literally first class; on earth I had to count pennies and find cheap places to stay. While I was disembarking in Singapore I started chatting with a buxom blonde American girl in the arrivals lounge, and when I said I thought I'd spend a few days in town before moving on to Vietnam she immediately invited me to stay in the bungalow she shared with her Chinese husband, a medical student. His family did not accept or acknowledge her, she was awfully lonely and she'd be grateful for company. Oh yes, and by the by, when we met, she'd been on her way back from Los Angeles where her sister had been the victim of a ritual murder. For the four days I was there she talked steadily, and I watched her knock back more than one hundred bottles of Coca-Cola. Unless she was sure there was plenty of coke in the ice-box for breakfast, she told me that she tossed and turned all night. It's common for Americans and the English to expatriate themselves to places where they can feed their addictions without trouble, though I'd not heard tell of Singapore being particularly liberal about Coca-Cola. But what made her an oddity in my collection of expats was that she had chosen her Chinese husband instead of an American suitor, she said, and come to live with him in Singapore, because his penis was small.

In Saigon they were selling black power symbols in the street market, and sealed packets of Park Lane cigarettes with filter tips that contained surely the strongest marijuana in the world. I smoked one in my hotel room, and when I came back to my senses the same rats were at play in the garden under my window only the moon had disappeared and it was time for lunch. A tough old sergeant getting drunk on the terrace of the Intercontinental

Hotel grumbled to me about how his scouts had to go out in the morning and collect the sentries who had had their throats cut from behind, the joint still clutched in their teeth. Vietnam was his third 'conflict', he called it, and when his boys asked him what the fuck they were doing in 'Nam, he didn't know what to tell them. Soon he was drunk to the point of passing out, whereupon two very young American soldiers came forward from the door.

'Excuse us, ma'am,' they said, and gently they lifted his arms over their shoulders so between them they could lead him away.

I was waiting on the terrace for a London journalist I knew who finally turned up with his Vietnamese friend, Monsieur Loc. M. Loc had a worldly tolerance that came within an inch of the British sense of humour at its best. His Buddha's calm was all the more impressive in a thin man, and a Catholic, as he turned out to be, with nine children at home. M. Loc, who made his living helping foreign journalists, took me on the back of his motor scooter and then by boat to spend a few days on an island in the Mekong where there lived some monks who had been praying for peace in relays every day, all day, for fifteen years.

'Hasn't done much good, has it, M. Loc?'

'One never knows, Mademoiselle Irma, how much worse things would be if they hadn't.'

The night we arrived on the island there was shelling on the nearby coast. Flashes of orange fire went off sporadically, and the rumbling of the big shells was organic and planetary. M. Loc and I leaned on the rail of the floating monastery, side by side, listening to war. Under his breath I heard him counting in French, and when I asked him why, he said he was calculating how much each boom, and pop, and rat-at-at-at was worth in piastres, and how much each piastre was worth in rice. Before Saigon fell, M. Loc and his entire family fled to France where, a friend told me, within a year he was dead of a heart attack. He had more heart than most; the attack must have been massive.

Australia arrived on schedule; Fiji on a Sunday, soon after; then, my first trip to California, and presto! the world had turned around under me, and there I was in Manhattan, staying with Irene. Since we'd last seen each other, she had become political. With all the purblind fervour of her Russian heart she was campaigning for a local congressional candidate against the devil incarnate. New layers of mess lay over the usual accretions in her flat. Pickles, the scrofulous cat, burrowed dog-like into piles of placards and campaign buttons, and left turds in odd hidey-holes. Young activists came and went all day long and into the night asking for instructions and materiel; they adored Irene, and she loved them back, teased them, pampered her favourites and fed them bortsch, pancakes and take-away pizzas out of greasy boxes that accumulated under the kitchen table. Nobody was awfully interested in where I'd been. Only one or two of the kids sat still for my thoughts on a war that was taking on its own life. Perhaps all wars do. They looked bemused when I told them to forget their good guys and their bad guys, nobody from top brass to the lowest grunt knew who was who or what the hell was actually going on.

'Brace yourselves,' I said, 'for trouble at home when it's all over. The only battle out there with any logic to it is between black and white Americans.'

They looked significantly at the glass of red wine I carried around between nightfall and bedtime, and told me again about their congressman. Irene rarely left the flat except to buy groceries and once or twice we went for dinner in a cheap and cheerful restaurant. A few months earlier she had consigned her mother to a nursing home run by Catholic nuns on the upper Hudson. The place was clean and cheap she said: 'And they'll let her play her piano.'

'Had she gone crazy, Irene?'

Irene shrugged: 'There's work to be done. And she was driving me crazy.'

New York's streets surged with their usual energy, filling my head with the roar of surf, night and day, and calling me out to play. But as soon as I was on the sidewalk letting myself be pulled along in the human current, I felt the weight of the whole world dragging at my back, and New York suddenly felt too small to hold me and much more constricting than I remembered. I missed the paucity of abrasive encounters on the pavement, I missed the choice not to overhear strange women in front of me discussing their hysterectomies, the silence of the street-crazed, the shortage of pedigree killer dogs. I missed 'sorry, sorry, sorry' at the accidental touch of an elbow. I missed untroubled eye contact. I longed for disinterested spontaneity and for privacy in a crowd. I missed London. And equally I missed proximity to a continent full of traditions and practically free of fundamentalism or religiosity.

When I stepped out of the airport bus into London, 'the smoke', after my long, lone, celibate journey around the world, my head was full to bursting with unsorted impressions I couldn't wait to develop, frame and put in place.

'Back already?' said my landlord, who happened to be going out as I arrived.

Not bothering to unpack, I raced out first to buy a paper, for local news and to check out the by-lines of people I know. The answering machine was yet to be invented; I was on the phone to friends before I'd changed out of my travelling clothes.

'Back already?' they all said.

Tea suits London's pace, even the tea-bag is not strictly speaking 'instant' and requires a ritual to its brewing. I sipped my first decent cuppa in months and smiled out at Lansdowne Crescent: 'Back already?' I could hear it whisper. And I knew everything that happened to me in London thereafter was going to be relative only to itself. There were no more comparisons, no regrets, no mortal wanderlust: I'd been cured. For better or worse, probably 'til death us did part, I'd come home.

11

Merton High Street

When I saw Rhoda for the first time after my long journey around the world, she greeted me grandly as the all-knowing one would condescend from nirvana: 'You back already?'

We had not long to wait before both turning 35 within two weeks of each other; a necklace I'd bought for her in a Delhi market was still in the bottom of my bag. I was going to carry it home again. Rhoda had always looked much older than her age, time had caught up with her while I'd been away and she was momentarily in her prime, standing there plumply at the door. Behind her was my old flat, still looking as if she'd just moved in. A London woman friend was already there; the easy way she was sitting with her feet up on the battered sofa told me that in my absence she had become more Rhoda's friend, less mine. She flashed me a posh receptionist's smile. Sherman, formerly my big grey tom, had stayed in the Chelsea home he'd made his own, and he had become altogether Rhoda's cat. He gave me a wicked yellow wink from his old place over the threshold to the kitchen. The warmth of a homecoming traveller cooled on my skin.

The attack began before my coat was on a hanger. Tales and adventures bubbling to be told sank red-hot into memory. While I had been galloping the globe, my London women friends with Rhoda as their outrider had been galloping off to Hampstead where the analysts, lay-analysts and anti-analysts. Quickly, with a smile that was inside-out and kept the softer side for herself, Rhoda outlined for me the psychic progress she had made while I was gallivanting. The high point of her therapy had been a recollection of her birth so replete with sticky detail, her therapist told her he had encountered birth memory among his analysands countless times before, of course, but never one as profound as hers. I imagine that the memory of being born must rank in importance down around remembering a bad day in the departure lounge at Heathrow. And I probably said as much, because Rhoda turned away and exchanged a look of I-told-you-so with our friend.

'Self-knowledge becomes all knowledge,' pronounced she, and the other woman nodded.

Before I could object or say a word, Rho plucked a postcard out of thin air it seemed, and waved it imperiously. I recognised it as one I'd sent months before from Sydney. Over the years, in Spain and Greece and aboard *Stormsvalla*, it became a standing joke between us that Rhoda never bought a swim-suit, she always ended up with mine and I had to buy a new one: Hank called it 'a bathing-suit graft'. On the card I'd written that I had chosen not to swim in the shark-infested bay of Sydney because: 'If a shark takes me, what would you do for a swim-suit?'

'Your problem . . .' Rhoda began, still flapping the card like a duellist's glove.

My problem was that I thought of others, and specifically of her, in terms of their need for me. That was only the preamble, there was lots more I cannot remember delivered in a jargon that later would be called psycho-babble. What was confronting me was in fact the first twitch in a movement of knowing-it-all that was going to dominate middle-brow London society for the next fifteen years or so, creating emotional carnage at dinner-parties, and promulgating unkindness, especially among us women, that can be found to this day in some retrograde households.

'But . . .' I started to defend myself.

Many years were to pass before I learned that there is no

defence against a middle-aged woman, even myself, who thinks she knows it all.

'Tip-ee-kull,' Rhoda crooned, and exchanged nods with the other woman. 'You send me 99 standard cards and then repudiate the only one that means anything. You're so out of touch with yourself, you don't even know you intended this card to hurt me. You never know what you don't want to know. That's your problem. I've been your patsy in the past. But not any more. I'm not here for you. I'm here for me.'

'You hurt Rhoda,' said the other woman, 'to make her hurt you to punish you for hurting her.' She looked at the boss for approval. 'You're like an unsighted woman driving at night without any headlights.'

'Redundantly blind,' I said.

'Don't be smart,' commanded Rhoda.

The postcard was a curtain warmer. Recrimination and criticism and character slaughter followed, every word delivered from an unassailable position of fake clinical detachment. Faults and wrongs were cited all the way back to my choice of *Tristram Shandy* for my third-year paper at Barnard: 'an undemanding frivolity' according to Rhoda.

'Your problem was you wanted to give your parents the child they wanted,' the friend said helpfully.

'One good turn deserves another,' I replied, game but growing weak.

Then, at a nod from Rhoda, in a choreographed movement, they both planted themselves side by side near the door, like a pair of centurions blocking my escape. What Rhoda said they wanted me to do was stand with my back to them and let myself fall into their arms. It was an exercise in trust, endorsed by their therapist.

'If you can learn to trust me,' Rhoda said, 'you're on the road to understanding me.'

By that time I'd rather have trusted a rattlesnake. The on-slaught had been premeditated and rehearsed. In my absence I had been dissected and reassembled as the bad big sister, the treacherous friend; I was all their hateful mothers. Tears had started banging away behind my eyes.

Some of us are born with a better sense of who we are not than who we are. On the way back to Notting Hill Gate, remembering, I touched the new bruises to see how sensitive they were.

'No. No. No. That isn't me,' I concluded.

All knowledge became self-knowledge. Each hurt subsided to an ache, and the wounds healed in due course into hairline scars. One thing I learned there that night alone in a carriage on the Circle Line: I am not one of those who respond to insult with anger. I am hurt, and in the past deeply hurt. People of my temperament become if not indifferent to disappointment, then certainly ironically inured to it. In that, I think I must be rather typically English. A few days later Rhoda did what furious and unprincipled children do: she killed me. A little. As far as her own universe was concerned, her universe of one – the universal Rhoda – I was dead. Phone calls stopped. My letters from over the years she returned to me in five shoe-boxes. For reasons that much later became evident, Rhoda never went back to live in the United States; she stayed in London, but she and I did not speak again for seven years.

Our youth had been prolonged by the nature of the times, and it was drawing to a close. Ageing is mostly a matter of becoming 'more so'. Rhoda, like the rest of us only at a quicker tempo, had begun becoming 'more so'. It's a process more apparent in women than men, because they have more to lose. We clever, assertive, mostly childless London women on the edge of middle age were just starting to surrender favours: first, bloom and easy attraction, verve, amorous choices; soon fertility would go, then lust, resilience, cherished opinions, secret ambitions, and finally, they tell me, wit and hope, until what's left in the end is an essence of us, not much more than a perfume, sweet or foul, that lingers on for a while, and blows away. Not very long after the Chelsea blitzkrieg, the friend who witnessed it, ever my friend, fell out with Rho too, and said of her: 'She is evil.' In a way, that was a pretty accurate assessment. What's left, like what began, is pure and simple.

While Rhoda had demonised me in my absence, Tony, the man who was my lover when I left to see the world had done the opposite. I was surprised that after so long an absence he wanted to resume the relationship, and I went back into it because I could say that 'he was a very nice man', and with those words, 'a nice man', repudiate love. Besides he could be a real pain in the ass, and what was terminally more to the point, he had the knack of making me one too. I loved – and I still do – his stubborn devotion to Art. We were both more bohemian than conventional, more hippies than swingers; and, oh, I don't know: I *was* 35. Tony rented an old church hall to use as a studio in an area of south London that was so unprepossessing and so very far removed from its considerable historical grandeur that I was probably the first and only American to hear of Merton High Street, let alone to get a kick out of it. While Tony dashed among the three or four huge paintings he was working on simultaneously in the main body of the chapel, I tapped away in the small office cum vestry. Whatever sect had once used the place for worship was austere: no pews, no pulpit, or niches, or altars – only a shaky gallery along the blind side of the room, and a few biblical quotations painted freehand on the walls. 'Drink ye all of it; for this is my blood . . .' was the first thing we saw upon entering in the morning. Windows set too high to see through let in muffled street noises from outside, sunlight shining through the dirty panes sent down long golden streaks that in classical paintings presage a supernal messenger. One of our friends in pursuit of his fortune bought a dozen old American pinball machines from a defunct penny arcade, and Tony was storing them until he found a buyer. During breaks from work we used to play them, our cups of tea precariously balanced on the frames. The best of the lot was called 'Central Park'; it featured an organ-grinder who walloped his monkey with a mallet at every new 1000 points. On the wall over where it stood was written: 'Death through sin . . .'

Merton High Street provided my only period as a more or less conventional significant half. Indeed never before or again did the slightest hint come my way of what it's like to be married: the strangely uncomplicated and slightly uneasy use of 'we' for everyday business; the slow-growing security, safe and claustro-phobic, of working in a team of two; the protective colouring generated by a couple in society, so common and ubiquitous that it is noticeable mostly by its absence when it has ended. And the daily routine that so quickly becomes one's own, yet remains someone else's. At night, we'd stock up on groceries in the run-down local shops or pick up some take-away from the Indian restaurants and then pile into Tony's yellow car, parked as usual nose-down on a hill so it would start, and drive back to the leafy comforts of Lansdowne Crescent. There we'd have a drink alone or with friends, some dinner, then to bed and probably make love; if we didn't, no big deal. There was always tomorrow.

The high streets of London before the big chain stores homo-genised them were a catalogue of outmoded good ideas and services that had grown out of special local requirements. Merton High Street still had an ironmonger called 'The Ironmonger': more dust than metal, it was hanging on selling nails, screws, hip-baths, galvanised buckets and braided mops. A sign in Letraset over the old cash register read: 'We have mousetraps'. There was a café a few doors down where working men scoffed eels and mash, and across the street a chip shop sold saveloy sausages, cod's roe or fish and chips wrapped in *The Times* for class, or sometimes the *Daily Mirror* for you-know-what. I liked the penny-bun look of Merton High Street's bakery and hated the lardy taste of what they sold. Tins of beans bought at the corner shop had to be washed before we opened them at home or dust landed in the pot. A big park was not far away and there were side streets with houses of character; it was the very ordinary *Londonishness* of Merton High Street, however, that made it romantic for an expatriate who was still finding novelty and glamour in the workaday ways of her adoptive city, even those which someday she'd know enough to avoid: Christmas panto-mimes, for instance, and north London dinner-parties. At lunch-time we sometimes went for a beer to the local pub. In the faded, oaken silence of the public bar the old regulars downed pints and puffed the cigarettes held perpetually between their stained, clubbed fingers. Their womenfolk preferred the lounge bar and shots of gin with sweet fizzy mixers. In the summer they wore pink cardies over cotton prints in matronly sizes that were sold at 'Betty's' in the high street. 'Something fierce . . .' they said about whatever the weather was doing: raining, sleeting or hotting up in summer.

Practically everywhere in the world except England the dream of owning one's bit of land is part of a yokel's creed. Far and away the majority of city dwellers on this planet are happy living in rented flats; only Londoners feel a gut-driven urge to install themselves and their families in houses that they own. Thanks to London being a collection of villages, each with a high street, and because it is a rare capital that attaches no great shame to its suburbs, it has been feasible here for a moderately well-off person to purchase a whole house and garden all for his lonesome within hailing distance of Big Ben. In principle the idea of owning my own patch is appealing and very close to my shtetl heritage. But it does mean that like countless other working English men and women I am bound to pay off a mortgage instead of paying rent: we London householders, in other words, are all solidly in debt. Being in debt is a classic English tradition that goes way, way back; a gentleman's financial worth on these islands has generally been judged less by what he earns than by how much his expectations allow him to borrow. This standard English upper- and middle-class measure of prosperity started to be seriously democratised in the 1970s when even lowly single women and freelance writers like me were allowed to go heavily into debt. By the 1980s towering mortgages and overdrafts were beginning to spread themselves dangerously thin. As congenial as I find most aspects of my London life, there are one or two that continue to get me down: whelks and debt are two English customs that give me sleepless nights – I have never quite overcome my Jewish and American squeamish reluctance to indulge in either of them. More times than I can count over the years in London I have awakened in a cold sweat frantically juggling sums, or sometimes wondering why on earth I thought it necessary to try again, in spite of experience and the tenets of ancient faith, to digest fish-flavoured elastic bands.

As the 1970s got underway, most of the people I knew who were in their early to middle thirties were about to become that local urban phenomenon known as 'first time buyers'. And so was I. But in my case buying a house was the corollary to another decision so much more important than anything I had ever done that strictly speaking it was not a decision at all. Or if it was a decision, then it was one that decided me. A few months before I took off around the world, a Sunday paper published an article citing my reasons for never having a baby – over-population of the planet, uncertain future of humanity, brutish temper of mankind, the transcendent love of children as opposed to narrowly loving one's own child – all eminently sensible reasons to remain childless, and yet, in a notebook I kept just over a year later when Tony and I were on holiday in Greece, there are two lists of names, one for girls headed 'Hannah', and the other starting with 'Amos'.

'Thank God you changed your mind,' my son said when I showed him the lists. 'Can you imagine what the boys at school would have done with "Amos"?'

Whatever I'd written in the paper or thought I believed to be true, I was bound for duty – beautiful, humane, intelligent duty – and also for the sacrifice of more space, more opportunity, more love than one woman strictly needed. At last the time had come to move out of the centre of my world: I'd outgrown universal Irma. The nursery was no longer furnished for me. To have a child was not a decision I made consciously. As I said, it was deciding me. I was being decided. And life was never the same again. Along with things I could spare, I sacrificed a friend or two.

'I just can't hack it,' Irene said.

My son was about eight months old, it was our first trip to the States together, and ostensibly Irene was referring to a wet nappy I'd left carelessly in the usual mess of stuff on her bathroom floor. However I suspect it was a mother, any mother, in particular me as mother, she couldn't hack. Through an intermediary she offered to return the letters I'd written to her over the years. I said no, and wrote a final letter to tell her I'd think of her as a friend whether she wanted me to or not. Years later I heard she moved in the first wave of older drop-outs to Vermont. Even after more than twenty years, I still think of Irene as my friend, mischievously: it was the last thing in the world she wanted me to do.

Flexible time, money enough to live on, a London roof bought and mostly paid for: these were my priorities before it was going to be fair to make a little stranger welcome in my life. Conveniently, IPC folded a project I'd been editing and I jumped at the chance to take a small pay-off and go freelance, instead of back on the staff of the ailing *Nova*. Going freelance meant opting out of the Fleet Street hierarchy: working without an expense account, without a secretary or assistants, without camaraderie and gossip, free phones, stamps, stationery, and without paid permission to waste time. Lillian was particularly adamant that she thought I was doing the wrong thing. In Lil was a temperament made to order for office life: practically every move of hers was defensive, she had no scruples about small pieces of forgery, pilfering or minor fraud, she preferred enclosed spaces but hated home, she drove, she didn't mind showing underlings the rough of her temper; free from restrictions and routine, her habits became self-destructive. With the best intentions Lil tried to dissuade me from a path that for her would have led to fatal self-indulgence. I, on the other hand, become defensive only as part of a team: I am fussy to the point of superstition about my tools, I walk a lot, love my home, talk to myself, and suffer fools sadly; only in company do my habits become self-destructive. All in all I am shaped by nature as a journeyman scribbler and born to work freelance.

A few weeks before I went freelance Angelica was admitted to a private clinic for routine tests. Her first night there she awakened late, ripped off her nightgown and ran naked and screaming through the corridors. Lil couldn't hide pride as she told me that when the matron tried to stand in Angelica's way, the frail little old lady had picked the younger woman up bodily and hurled her against the wall.

'We are not equipped to deal with cases of this nature . . .' the chief administrator wrote on the letter Lil showed me. The clinic shipped Angelica home immediately and she had no recollection at all of what had taken place.

'Bad dream . . .' I said.

We both knew there was more to it. But I told myself that Chris took good care of Angelica, and the house; he cooked, cleaned and mended Lil's clothes while she was out at work. The unorthodox union between a man who slept only with men and a woman who fell in love only with women was working. Lil was slowly continuing to shed pounds, and when she complained about his extravagance and his tendency to tell tales, it was with the note of gruff affection she had used since the old days with Brigitte. During a sneaky trip across the Channel, she and Christopher had discovered a derelict property in the north of France they dreamed about doing up as a weekend hide-away for gay couples. The photograph of papa in the silver frame had blabbed to Angelica where to look for Lillian's bank statements, and where to find Brigitte's letters; mercifully, it wasn't in on the French project.

I calculated that I needed three or four pieces a week to support a mortgage and a baby. From the beginning and thanks to having been a *Nova* regular with a familiar by-line there was freelance writing enough to keep me hopping. Invitations started coming to appear on television and radio panel-shows too, which is a much easier way to make money than writing. Generally, I was asked to discuss 'female' issues: was the reformed abortion law working? The reformed laws regarding homosexuality? How about that quirky movement in America called 'women's lib'? Could men and women be friends? Whither marriage? Monogamy: manmade or natural? Nudity: art or prurience? Maternity: design or destiny? Sometimes they wanted me to talk about books, films and light or seasonal topics: New Year's resolutions: made to be broken? Can we live without lies? Royalty: past, present, or future?

From the here and now I can see that London was toying with the idea of making me a local celebrity. That it did not quite happen was nobody's fault but my own: I had the chance and I muffed it. I doubt very much the chance to be a celebrity would have come my way in any city other than London. In Paris, local celebrities take themselves very seriously and if they are celebrated for being funny, they are clowns rather than wits. Off-stage their appearance is solemn, even morose. Paris also celebrates professional intellectuals. Eastern European cities do too, or used to, only in Paris intellectuals were better dressed, and most of them were Communists. Celebrities out of America's great fame-pool, Hollywood, are not strictly speaking local: they flash across the whole world with the vivid life-span of butterflies Actors there do not becomes celebrities for their acting, not really; they are celebrated for being at the forefront of their established categories: blonde bombshell, for instance, sultry brunette, he-man, twisted nut-case, California surfer, laconic cowhand, funny fat man and so on. Although there is a 'Great Actor' category of Hollywood stardom, if a part comes along that threatens a celebrity's established position – his 'image' – then a talented, ego-blighted English actor has to be found to fill the role: Sheriff of Nottingham, not Robin Hood. As for New York, it takes to its big, nostalgic heart the old stars, women in particular, who have been practically forgotten everywhere else. Retrospectives, revivals and farewell performances are perpetual in New York and geriatric celebrities are more likely there than anywhere else to find a grateful audience. Otherwise, though New Yorkers say and sing 'if you make it there you'll make it anywhere', the fact is the place is full of local celebrities who hardly dare leave town except for the Hamptons or the Vineyard. London's local celebrities are parochial, too. They emerge from politics and sport, and a little less mannishly out of television and print journalism. Media London is a cannibal mother, creating from within itself a multitude of wiseacres upon which it then feeds, thus, many local celebrities make themselves known mainly by interviewing each other.

In 1972 I was offered a shot at the biggish-time when the BBC asked me to present *Film '72*, a weekly TV review of new movies along with celebrity interviews. From the beginning I was twitchy, miserable, badly turned out, bad at the role and incidentally, I was pregnant. When at last the thirteen weeks of ordeal was over, I took my successor out for a drink. He was an eager, fresh-faced young chap called Barry Norman.

'You won't be able to go into a local shop without some twit asking you what Gene Hackman is really like? Once they start seeing you on the box, you bloody belong to them: your butcher, your VD doctor, your postman – you're a celebrity, and they don't let you forget it.'

'I'm going to love it,' he said.

Love it he did, and that's why he was good at the job. He is a bright man, however, and in due course, I suspect, he started to love it less. Celebrities are fixed in the public eye, they cannot grow or experiment, or change a hair for us, not if they care for us: not if they want to stay celebrities. The time has to come when the only way a celebrity can stay celebrated is to start imitating his past self long after the initial inspiration has faded, and that is what freezes the soul and can destroy him. Fortunately the English have a rare gift for mimicry, and there is always at least one professional mimic who is himself a celebrity but who also acts a sort of Geiger counter for the others. As soon as any public figure has reached the point of imitating himself to a dangerous degree, that is precisely when the mimic starts to imitate him, too.

Very soon after her short stay in a nursing home Angelica started leaving the gas on without lighting the cooker; she lost the house keys too, and had been brought back by the police who found her wandering and confused a mile or more from the flat. Because of her fitful rages none of the residential homes Lil applied to in suburban London was willing to take her, and finally she had to settle for a place in the geriatric ward of a large mental hospital in the far south of the city. The last time I saw Angelica she was in the hospital's conservatory and I was standing well back out of sight behind the glass partition that separated it from the main body of the building. Tiny Angelica was slumped in her chair like a sleepy child. Lillian was sitting next to her, and for twenty minutes or more I'd been watching her hand-feeding Angelica fairy cakes, one by one, out of a box on her lap. A middle-aged woman in a white coat appeared at my side; the badge on her pocket said she was a resident psychiatrist.

'Look at that,' she said, her tired face suddenly radiant, 'as much good we try to do our patients, in the end, love is the cure.'

The drugs they'd given Angelica to keep her quiet had dried her out completely, and her dressing-gown was covered with crumbs that were dropping steadily from the corner of her mouth. Dazed and obedient she tried to swallow the ashes her daughter was stuffing into her mouth. Whatever it was we were watching it was not love, and it was time to put a stop to it.

12

Shepherd's Bush

'You'll find,' Donald told me before my first trip to London, 'that Englishmen in general are better at breakfast than bed.'

It's true that Englishmen are not at their best in love. Are any men, or women, at their best in love? But Englishmen don't even try to be. They are quick and verbal except in love, and good for a laugh all too often in love. The Englishman is made as other men. He lusts. He loves. He suffers. But he has inherited a tireless sense of the absurd which is one gauge of human intelligence that at the same time makes him unusually susceptible to embarrassment. No activity of humankind contains as great a potential for every sort of embarrassment as making love, particularly for a bloke, poor brute, stuck with flashy genitalia that can't be trusted to keep a secret, let alone keep faith. If Don Juan's sense of the ridiculous had extended to himself, he would have headed straight for England, used his credentials to join a men's club in London, found a wife of good breeding stock to whom he could be carelessly faithful while exhausting his excess ardour in fox-hunting and single malt whisky: no operas, no epics, no risk of disaster. Compounding the perils of performance to a man's dignity, and the possibility of crude comparison with other men, is the dreaded fact that love by and large in London as in other cities continues even now to be made with a member of the opposite sex whose standards, critical requirements and satisfaction remain a mystery, in spite of the way she will go on and on about them in words as shrill and incomprehensible as one of those feverish tongues of the desert.

If London has a true antipodes it is Tokyo: two cities poles apart and in ways similar, like distorted reflections of each other. The traveller cannot walk straight into London or Tokyo without putting a foot wrong: both cities drive on the left, both cities have resident Royals and both cities have to be learnt. Perhaps it's the isolation of island nations and their strictly limited space that exaggerates respect for privacy, and makes islanders hyper-sensitive to shame. Japan's protocol and class-system are much more complex and rigid than Britain's ever were, I guess because the Japanese did not sail out to colonise the globe; they stayed home for centuries perfecting their manners. On visits to Japan, and reading Japanese literature, I have the impression that codes and courtesies and class structures fixed there to keep highly-strung people from killing each other in a small space divided by paper walls, extended to intimate sexual relations too. Englishmen, however, were constantly rushing around all over the place in olden days, leaving their women to stew alone; they found the whole sex-thing-or-whatever too explosive and slippery and hag-ridden to control and preferred to abandon the beastly business to luck and conscience behind walls of stone.

'It's not like Paris,' said a French friend after we had been walking around central London and passed a lot of men who had given her the once-over. 'In Paris, when a man looks, you know exactly what he wants. There are rules. There's a form. But when the roast-beef looks at me, I don't know what he wants. Does he? Is it that here anything goes?'

The French have devoted a lot of attention to deciding exactly where they stand sexually, and have made it a point of honour to know what's expected of them: discretion, for example, tested techniques of arousal, contained satisfaction, waxed legs for women, a trouser-press for men. An Englishman, however, em-barking on sex finds himself in lawless territory where no matter how heavily armed is his amour proper, he puts it at risk, and all the more, if he comes from the educated middle class. No doubt, a lot will change as the great boarding-schools of England become co-educational and the sexes mix together from an early age; perhaps someday Englishmen will be as arrogant and offhand and choreographed in sex as Latin lovers in general, or as goal-orientated as American men. Meanwhile, in my experience over the past three decades, boys from good English schools continue to grow up into pretty good company at breakfast. Unfortunately when it comes to making love the educated Englishman's disastrous sense of the absurd is often compounded by poetry. Poetry is as lust-threatening as irony; together they can paralyse a man's libido. Poetry expects too much of love, and irony stops short at too little. Much twaddle has been written about the homosexuality instilled in English public-school boys. In fact the dominating quirk that Englishmen of every class have in common is not homosexuality, it is lifelong prurience (nudge-nudge) about the naughty bits, the dangly bits, the dirty bits. Salacious voyeurism is an inversion of prudery, another expression of embarrassment, and about as sexy as a short fat comic in drag.

Anyone who has ever tried to come to grips with a British Rail timetable knows how fiendishly able Englishmen are to obfuscate the simplest issues and sidestep a straightforward statement. Aside from prurience, alcohol, trace perversions and speedy withdrawal, the English lover uses a crab-like circumlocution, a sort of scuttling at the most basic declaration, which also serves to confuse amorous predators of the opposite sex.

'There's something quite interesting I want to say to you,' said the handsome Londoner. 'Well . . . no . . . it's quite boring really.'

We were sitting in the garden of my house in Shepherd's Bush early on a bright summer morning, drinking tea.

'Oh well, I don't know,' he said. 'Maybe not . . .'

We sat in silence for a while. The giant pear-tree in the garden abutting on mine was in fruit, the four daughters of an Indian family nearby were picking the tiny hard pears; they flitted from branch to branch in saris that were bright as birds. By nightfall the air would zing with the smell of simmering chutney. For a moment I forgot where I was. The Englishman sighed, looked into his teacup and grimaced painfully.

'Er–um, would you have such a thing as a spoon?' he asked.

Everywhere I looked were Englishmen; shy and sly they looked back at me. As do all other inbred islanders they fell broadly into physical types: sandy Scots, swaggering Vikings with thick necks; whey-faced Irish liars or too, too handsome blue-eyed Irish liars; foxy Londoners, tall crop-headed youngsters with long eyelashes, cocky London strutters or lean good suits with silky hair who favour neurotic women; and an unexpected dark and curly strain of British male with the cautious eyes of a shipwrecked sailor. Naturally I fell in love with Englishmen. Needs must. Thus it happened in due course that I had an English child, a Londoner, whose only complaint about the circumstances of his birth was that on weekends from our garden we could hear the crowd at Loftus Road football ground rumbling like a distant surge of testosterone, and the boy was condemned by geography to support Queens Park Rangers football team.

My son's father-to-be, Tony, was a partner in house-hunting, yet not. In many ways Tony was precisely the Artist with a capital 'A' my generation of long-haired Barnard girls had long, long ago admired breathlessly. He mistrusted all conventional impulses, he still does, and not least the one towards bourgeois nesting. But time had driven me into port and was storming at the windows of the nursery. The single adventure I could imagine was the most ordinary one in the world. Tony made it clear from the start that the house was in every practical sense going to be all mine, and that was better than all right with me.

Before setting out I considered broadly where I wanted to live by compass points. North was upward, trendy and ever-so pleased with its liberal self. East London was mysterious and authentic, and I'd live there now but at the time it was too exotic for my purposes. As for the south, though I know it is full of unmined treasures, it was remote and badly served by public transport. So like countless intrepid Americans before me I headed due west to find a home. Landsdowne Crescent was out of my league when it came to buying property, and so were the streets around Notting Hill Gate and Holland Park down the road. The gateway from Holland Park into Shepherd's Bush to the west is a roundabout, a railway bridge and a common, that altogether serve as London's answer to the Donner Pass: many land-hungry pioneers heading west take one look at Shepherd's Bush Green, and turn back. Once a year the circus comes to the green, and the roar of homesick tigers gives pause in the surrounding pubs, and tacky hamburger bars, and own-brand supermarkets. When the big top moves on, it leaves behind steaming elephant turds to further demoralise plant life already dwarfed and stifled by the fumes of London traffic. The green used to have a public loo for men, too, that looked so cute and cosy I mistook it for a park-keeper's lodge, and would have quite fancied the idea of living in it. The council had it boarded up not too long ago, as councils around London have many similar cottage-style men's loos in which actors and politicians used to be regularly arrested for soliciting. From the green there diverge two major roads forming a roughly triangular island, about six or seven miles long, of terraced homes, ranging from substantial buildings grown shabby to modest small houses built for factory and railway workers in the late nineteenth century, when the entire area was converted to industry from farms and brick-fields. In the early 1970s Hammersmith like many other London boroughs had started to sell off empty property in danger of dilapidation. The estate agent for Hammersmith, of which Shepherd's Bush makes the northern sector, was too busy to sh properties, so he gave Tony and me the keys along with available addresses in my price-range, and we set o second-storey men to case them. Looking for a was not unlike looking for love: a sensible per that perfection is academic and settled for course love being a form of madness, nobody who's in it is sensible. House-hunting, on the other hand, was relatively cut and dried.

The very first house we saw would have suited me just fine: rooms were bright, the roof was solid, plumbing intact, and through the back windows I saw a garden brushed with early spring green. It wasn't a palace, true enough, but when have I imagined myself to be a princess? It was sound, it was comfortable: it would do. In my mind I had started decorating the kitchen when a thump on the stairs behind me made me whirl around. There stood a crone, her nose and chin nearly of a piece.

'You'll never get me out of here,' she cried. 'Never. Never!'

She banged her stick on the floor and came a step closer. A smell of flowers rotting in unchanged water was coming off her in waves. I backed away.

'The Hun couldn't move me. And neither can you. I'm a sitting tenant, I am. And I'll bloody sit here, I will. When you take me out, it'll be feet first.'

She must have been close to a century and would not much longer take up space in any house outside the coffin. But flashing from her eyes and electrifying her hair into a quivering white halo was malice, undiluted, that would be bound to live on as a presence long after her bones had turned to dust. I called Tony and quickly we moved along to the second address on the list, three streets closer to central London. It was smaller than the other, and smaller than most on the list, though larger than it appeared to be from outside. The instant I crossed the threshold into the entrance hall I loved the house. While Tony poked around the upstairs rooms – there were three of them, the one on the first landing no bigger than a box-room – I stood alone in a double room divided by folding doors on the ground floor. Bay windows opened on to a small front yard, and a big window at the back looked down on an overgrown weed-pit, facing southwest. Window to window, light filled the room with golden dust. To ~~surprise~~ I found I was holding my breath. The future was humming through the house, and me; or it might have been the past. Overhead, the ceiling was edged with a scrolling plaster bas-relief that seemed from where I stood to illustrate the bed-time story I liked best when I was little, about a traveller wearing magic boots who comes home with tales to tell.

The little house cost £5,000: I raised the £500 deposit that was required; the remaining £4,500 was a mortgage. It sounds a small sum now, but in 1970 it was more than enough to make sleepless nights for a freelance writer in a town that averages two dozen reporters to every story. The house had been empty for some time so I was spared the agony of dickering with resident owners while they stalled, awaiting their own removal to a new place on the dreaded chain. Hammersmith council's sales-staff in those days was composed of honest and well-intended amateurs, one of whom told me he thought I'd be 'good for the neighbourhood'. With him on my side I didn't fear being pipped at the gate by someone offering more than the price we had settled for: 'gazzumping' was the made-up word for this new cause of heartbreak in property-mad London. During the weeks while the paperwork was being processed, I took an hour or so off whenever I could to visit Shepherd's Bush and learn more about what was going to be the most important place in the world for the next fifteen years of my life, and the first fourteen of my son's life.

Sometimes to this day when I come back from a trip, I'll jump into a taxi at the airport and with all the heat of homecoming in my heart, I hear myself start to ask the driver to take me to Ellingham Road, Shepherd's Bush, even though I haven't lived there for ten years. Only yesterday was the first time in a decade I have been back 'down the Bush'. It's not because I left angry that I stayed away so long: I left when it was over and until yesterday, I had no reason to go back. Apparently not many Londoners have a reason to go where I used to live, or why has London Transport curtailed the number 12 bus that used to travel from the West End straight down the Uxbridge Road? Thus they have effectively dissected my old neighbourhood from mainstream urban life. If I still lived there, I'd have fought like fury to keep that bus route, the way a band of us fought for our avenue of lime trees back in the mid-70s when the council wanted to cut them down because they dripped sap on parked cars. We collected signatures, we canvassed, we lectured, we scolded, we bored and chivvied, we pleaded, we wrote endless letters to the press and our MP. Why, I even swore I'd chain Ingrid to a tree – she was our Swedish au pair – at the first sight of woodsmen with axes. The day the council voted on the trees I was interviewing a dim-witted movie-star on location in San Francisco. At the end of a pier into the bay near where they were filming, I finally found a working telephone and got through to a neighbour in Ellingham Road where it was early evening. Two hundred or so California sea-lions basking under the pier looked up at my 'Yippee!' because a dozen lime trees had been spared, half a world to the east.

From the Underground station at Shepherd's Bush Green it's a short walk to the market and seven blocks further to the familiar turn-off for home. Shepherd's Bush market was so badly bombed during the war the council was going to shut it down permanently, until the stallholders dug it out of the rubble with their own hands, and had it back in business within days. The market has expanded recently and a marked West Indian presence gives it a new beat and colours. Fifteen or twenty years ago Shepherd's Bush was one of the favourite London street markets for the womenfolk of visiting Arabs; liveried chauffeurs used to drive up in long silent cars and drop them off to shop. Faces hidden behind satin grilles, children clutching at their robes or pushed in prams by servants, the Arabian wives emanated a lot less defensive hostility 'down the Bush' than they did at Harrod's. They haggled cheerfully over spices, vegetables, fluffy seat covers for the toilet, mountains of pink nylon underwear, ornate lamps with many bulbs, pointy shoes and gaudy plates. Halfway down the market was a pet shop where we always paused so my son could flirt with the kittens, and at a stall on the corner of the Uxbridge Road was a greengrocer who called me 'luv', 'dahlin', 'swede-art', and who gave Marc unwashed apples to eat in the push-chair on the way home. His stall is there now, kept by a woman who has the shrewd, kind face I remember; she must be his daughter. None of the big high-street chains have bothered to invade the Uxbridge Road, so there are no common London logos. What with the loss of the old double-decker red bus and not a black cab in sight, the walk to my old home hardly felt Londonish at all, or even very English, particularly on a summer day when the breeze was delivering smells from hotter countries. Middle Eastern tea-rooms, Greek kebab houses, soul food, even a Thai restaurant, have opened on my route where formerly there were no eating places to speak of, only a take-away chicken shop that appeared one morning two streets from our home; by nightfall the pavement outside was stained and slippery with grease. It still is. In the 1980s, a French bistro was started up not far away and my mother, who happened to be visiting at the time, wondered hopefully if it was a sign the neighbourhood was improving. It wasn't. The proximity of the BBC's TV Centre and rumoured plans for its expansion made local estate agents happy to think that media yuppies would colonise the Bush. They didn't. Most of them stayed put in north London, the others bypassed us and headed straight for Chiswick or Hammersmith on the river. Shepherd's Bush had the distinction of being passed over by some very grand folk indeed: every so often I'd be waiting on a traffic island to cross the Uxbridge Road, and find myself eyeball to eyeball with the Queen, only the window of her car between us as she was being hurried through the Bush to Windsor.

A bearded drunk sat with his back against the wall where Mr Patel used to have his supermarket. In my day, Mrs Patel would have been out there like a shot with her broom to brush him off her nice clean pavement. The off-licence is gone; the sub post office remains, but 'Owen, the Milk' went long before I did, and the video shop that replaced him is gone now too – the shop is to let. Past the next corner there once was a meeting hall in classical style that West Indians used to favour for weddings. Layers of confetti lay under its portico every Monday as if a multi-coloured blizzard passed through on Sundays. The hall was torn down about eighteen years ago and buddleia is overhanging the hoarding around the empty lot where it used to stand, so I guess all bruited plans for revitalising the area have yet to happen. My former newsagent is now a shop that sells parts of machinery to tall Jamaicans in dreadlocks. The only familiar business remaining on the street where I used to shop is the butcher. A lad in a straw hat and white apron was looking out of the big window and as I was passing he half-raised his hand in greeting. I had started to wave back before I realised he could hardly have been more than a toddler ten years ago when I moved away, and he couldn't know me from Adam.

The lime trees have grown to magnificence; they tower over the facing rows of terraced houses and lend them grandeur far beyond the style of any neighbouring streets. In general, Shepherd's Bush has not come up in the world; Ellingham Road, however, has not gone down. Yesterday, the blessed trees made a cool green corridor through the unseasonably hot afternoon. New cars lined both sides of the street but there wasn't a soul to be seen. I didn't need to check the doorbells to know that none of my former neighbours live there any more: designer blinds in the bay windows told me as much, and vases of store-bought flowers. Near the top of the street on the even-numbered side there lived an old couple who came to Ellingham Road when they were married and in fifty years had not gone away again, except him to war, not even as far as the West End more than half-a-dozen times on occasions of great national observance – a couple of royal funerals, a couple of coronations, VE Day, the Festival of Britain. After that they preferred to stay home 'down the Bush' watching it on telly. One day we heard that workmen insulating their roof discovered an unexploded bomb like a dotty heirloom in the attic. I asked the fireman who lived across the street in an odd-numbered house how on earth he thought anyone could have mended a roof, as the old folks must have needed to do after the Blitz, without checking first to see what had caused the hole in it?

'Probably in too much of a flaming hurry,' said the fireman.

The old couple's house has been divided into two flats with a smart double-entry hall. Where the fireman and his family used to live, a silver-grey Mercedes is parked outside the gate. Six doors further along tailor-made curtains open on a glimpse of parquet floor and Tibetan prayer rugs where Richie's mother raised three big sons alone, only one of them in Borstal, and Richie as bright and good as any friend Marc ever brought home for tea. And over every door in the street, including the one that used to be mine, is a burglar-alarm system. Twenty-five years ago, a few months after moving in, Tony and I went to Greece for a week while engineers had the floorboards up to install the central heating. Returning home I eagerly unlocked my very own front-door – it was red with a knocker in the shape of a treble clef – and saw that the place had been robbed, cleaned out of every last thing portable, it transpired, including a kitchen sink not yet plumbed in. I didn't cry or carry on, not even when I found my great-grandmother's seed pearls missing. As I saw it, until my arrival there nobody in living memory had installed central heating or been burgled. I was the thin end of a yuppie wedge into Ellingham Road, and the hearth gods had demanded propitiation.

Ellingham Road used to be practically a cul de sac, safe enough for my son and Richie and the others to play football in the street. At the far end it has been opened up since we moved away to make room for a low block of flats with balconies set stylishly at angles to each other across from the Infants' School in its boxy post-war building. From the study-bedroom that ran the width of my house on the second-floor, I sometimes paused in my work to listen to the children laughing and calling out each other in the playground. My desk was a trestle table with a green felt top, the telephone was bright green too. Our number was SHE-3874, but only for a few months before London went digital and 'SHE' for 'Shepherd's Bush' became '749'; if we lived there now, we'd have needed to add the unfashionable prefix '0181' a few years back when London phones became too numerous to count the old way. Along the wall facing the window I'd put up bookshelves from floor to ceiling and there were more shelves in the alcoves either side of the bed. The short wall at the foot of the room was covered in cork: no Proustian affinity – it served as a huge bulletin-board. On the day I have in mind, I was working on a piece about sexual jealousy (again!) for a women's magazine. Page one had been standing in the roller of my Olivetti long enough for the brewing and cooling of two cups of tea. A picture of Colette was tacked on the cork wall for inspiration, and I was studying her face – aged in the would, and the could, and oh, how admirably she did! – when the phone rang. A social worker attached to the local clinic was calling to tell me my test had come back and it was positive.

'Oh, I'm so happy you're happy,' she said. 'I can't tell you how happy I am you're happy! I was so afraid you wouldn't want it. You not being married, and all . . .'

Sitting on the low wall in front of the school, I looked at my old house diagonally across the street. Virginia creeper planted in 1978 when Marc was six, covered the front, draped the little balcony and fell back in a fringe over the bay windows downstairs. White venetian blinds were drawn tight where I'd had Canadian redwood slats. Obviously nobody was at home. Not that I would have knocked on the door, thank you very much – not in a million years. No matter how pleased the seller and buyer of a house both are with the deal, there is never love lost between them: it's a spiritual impossibility. Odds on the first thing my buyer did when he moved in was hack down the Empress rose I'd coaxed around the fence at the back. New owners can't wait to uproot the established garden. He has managed to grow a few flowers in the small front yard – no cats, I guess. I used to encourage my cats to decimate the front yard, hoping that way they'd leave the garden at the back alone.

A life can be told in cats: poets and other cat-loving fabulists are always doing it. Once upon a time, Hoi and Polloi, two Burmese blues, moved with their mistress, lady journalist and world-traveller, to Ellingham Road. They were the familiars of her sophisticated middle thirties. They photographed well. They were neutered. They were cool cats. In April, six months or so before a baby was due in the house, Hank turned up unexpectedly in London with his new American wife, and they came to stay for a while. One day, Hank carried home a stray kitten he'd found in the street. Hoi was no snob: when in the mood, he'd fetch a silver ball, walk out on a lead, and perform a few other common doggy tricks. It was Polloi who carried the weight and duty of the family's pedigee: he took one look at the flea-bitten urchin nosing his dish of freshly cooked lambs' hearts, and he was over the fence and out of sight. For hours we searched the neighbourhood, but there was not a sign of him until around tea-time there came a knock at the door. A stocky middle-aged man stood there in apparent distress.

'I'm so sorry . . .' he said.

He'd found my address on Polloi's collar. The cat had raced out of nowhere right in front of his car, and was in the back seat now in a bad way. If we wanted to take the poor thing to a Blue Cross clinic nearby, the stranger would be glad to give us a lift. Tony and I got into the back seat of the car. I took Polloi in my arms. He was breathing, there was no blood to be seen, but one side of his head was stoved in, and his eyes were cloudy and lopsided. The beat was running down inside his sturdy little body, and suddenly I knew full force what it meant to take on responsibility for another life. A divine creature was dying in my arms because I had failed him. Tony looked over at me.

'It's only a cat,' he said, and he laughed.

Probably it was a nervous laugh; my son's English father is not unkind, nor is he unfeeling: months later, the first time he held our baby in his arms, he trembled and was lit by wonderful emotions. Tony wasn't wrong to laugh; I wasn't right to cry. We were doing what we had to do. But there was no way two like us were going to make it together to the end.

Certain places are booby-trapped for memory, and the moment I got off the train yesterday at Shepherd's Bush for the first time in a decade I walked into a hail of debris from the past. Especially in Ellingham Road a bombardment of memories was all around me, and most of it hit home. There, across my path at a proud Burmese canter, went Hoi who had hated my pregnancy and was adopted by a friend in Chelsea where he led a style of life his poor brother would have loved. Rattling down the empty street I heard again the home-made cart in which the sons of Ellingham Road took turns pulling each other; it made a noise out of all proportion to its size. Richie's mum, a little the worse for sherry, used to storm out of her front door yelling: 'Put a bleedin' lid on it!' And then I'd lean out of my study window: 'Keep it down boys, please, I'm trying to work.' Before my mind's eye passed the neighbour's pear tree, the way it looked in blossom from my back garden, a spill from paradise. Fragments and splinters from the past were whizzing everywhere: the Victorian stone cat Don-Don gave me for the garden; my house-keys on a souvenir ring from Sydney that caught on the lining of my bag; the rat that got into Marc's room – the exterminator finally beat it to death with my tennis racket; the deep-fat fryer – had I really ever used so unwholesome a thing? – in which I used to make French-style chips for the boy. And ouch! I ducked a teaspoon – 'such a thing as a teaspoon' – blackened on its base. I had found it under the bed in the spare room after Hank and his wife moved out.

Being in a place of memories is like watching a sunset: there comes a point before the final blaze when enough is enough. I rose from the wall, dusted myself off and for one more time in my life, it was probably the last, I prepared to leave Ellingham Road. At the top of the street where it joins its neighbour, two boys were lounging against a parked car. They were about the age of Marc and Richie in the era of the noisy wagon. I smiled at them as I was passing.

'Oi!' one of them called after me. 'Got a ciggie on you?'

13

Ellingham Road

From a very early age I knew that nationalism was like twelve-times tables, bookshelves too high to reach, and in-store Santas with bad breath: a piece of grown-up fun-loathing expediency. By the time any bright child was ten or eleven, she had to see that the twelve-times table was an attempt to turn us all into wholesalers, top-shelf books were far and away the most diverting and educational, Macy's Santa was a dud, and human beings were born to the whole beautiful planet, not merely the flyspecks where they happened to pop out. Half a century on I haven't changed my mind. No emotional tie whatsoever holds me to any passport; the passport is a document of convenience, that's all it is, and when last year on the Ides of March I had myself naturalised as British it was because I was sick and tired of cooling my heels behind the entire Polish Symphony Orchestra in the non-European Community queue every time I came back from abroad. It was not to become a Britisher that I left my homeland, nor did I set out on my travels with the intention of becoming an expatriate. Even if I'd cared to be other than the nationality I was born to, expatriation could never be accomplished, nor will it ever be until we learn to travel backwards and correct the port of embarkation. Passports do not pertain: every traveller is on a lead attached to childhood, and it cannot stretch beyond an optimum point when the scales tip, and the balance of her love, her hope, and probably her livelihood too, reside no longer in the land of her birth, but where like a wind-driven seed she fell, blossomed and came to fruit. When I learned from Her Majesty's government that giving birth to an Englishman did not accord me the same cheap right of citizenship I'd have had for marrying one of them, I wanted to cry 'But I have not merely bedded in England, I have blossomed and bloody well fruited here too!'

On October 9th, 1972 I became the American mom of a baby boy whose first word was going to be 'Mum'. No passport on earth, or oath, or ersatz accent could make any alien mom more bona fide a Londoner than her very own little cockney's first 'Mum'. With Marc's birth I came as close to transplanting the past as anyone can, for I entered childhood again, this time in a foreign land where there were lullabies I'd never learned to sing, ancient games I didn't know how to play and a whole unknown body of literature: *Uncle Remus* was the bedtime treat where I'd grown up, not Enid Blyton; the guru of my childhood was Mark Twain, not C. S. Lewis. Fair enough, my son and I shared Alice and Toad of Toad Hall, but who in blazes was Postman Pat? I didn't like the look of him, nor of the old man who played knick-knack on kiddies' knees. To top off confusion, I had to agree with the mothers at Marc's nursery school when they complained that *Sesame Street*, wherever had come its inspiration, was disseminating questionable Americanisms: what was a 'zee' to me and mine, for instance? My baby boy's alphabet ended in 'zed'. As Marc progressed in school, the gap in our childhood experience did not narrow: what was the difference between A levels and O levels, 11-plus and GCSE? A 'Head Master' and a 'Head Teacher'? A 'Prefect' and a 'Head Boy'? Was 'prep' the same as homework? 'You just don't care, do you?' Marc said to me once, affronted, when I'd confused his sixth-form 'Open Day' with an American-style seniors' 'Field Day' which it turned out was more like an English 'Sports Day'. It wasn't that I didn't care; I cared. But like any old-timer learning a new language, my ear and my intellect had aged at a different rate and were out of kilter. As often as my son tried to explain to me the rules of Cricket, for example, my mind moaned 'Baseball', and turned away.

Marc was a babe in arms when Tony moved out altogether into a place of his own not far away, where very soon he was living with a calmer woman than I. Marc and Tony continued to see each other regularly, and do to this day. Looking back it is evident that our separation was always on the cards. I was not cut out for coupledom, and probably wouldn't have been a good wife to any man, let alone to one as diffident and critical as Tony. Loving as a wife was for me a condition of enforced idiocy and frustration. Half of 'we' in no time ceased to be I and became someone else's opinion, not even of me, of what someone else thought I ought to be. The more I struggled, the deeper I was stuck. I was suffocated and I hated it. On the other hand nurturing another person created to be set free, loving him with an open heart and hands and an open mind, loving as a mother, I mean, suited me very well. In an ideal world I would have given Marc a sibling or two. Perversely and hormonally-driven, I nevertheless continued to expect the mate to gallop in at last who would love me as myself, the way nobody ever had. Of course I was surprised to wake up alone late in life knowing that was how it was going to be. Any woman who fancies men and is attractive is bound to be surprised the first time she walks out of a party into the dark streets alone, looking for a taxi home. The end of carnal passion and daydreams is no immediate cause for celebration; how could it be? Gradually the sap has dried, the processes wound down, and she knows herself to be a coffin for small dead parts. But if she is an independent cuss with some imagination and chutzpah, then it can't be very long before the melancholy gives way to an emotion deeper than acceptance, and more positive, almost relief: never again to live up to anyone else's opinion, or what is more likely, live down to it. An end to heart-sapping obsessions and the humiliation of predictable disappointments. Extra hours in the day. No more swift kicks in the ego, or addling of the id, or decking out the libido in robes of state. She can like men and find interest in their company that no young female still with sex to grind ever could. I went into Ellingham Road as an expectant female in every sense; by the time I left, it was as a Cassandra for younger women.

The American vision of London is inspired by Dickens and Conan Doyle and old movies: the capital swirls up even now into the Yank's imagination out of a fog so thick that sneak thieves and footpads can go about their villainy as unremarked as croutons in pea-soup. Of course, it's not really like that, not any more. Yet Ellingham Road had been built in Victoria's London, and remnants of the era were still around when I moved in. Green belts and smoke-free zones had not yet been put into effect to clear the air, and I shall ever be able to boast that I had the thrill and honour of finding myself out and about during the last great classic fog to descend on London out of bygone days, smelling like a newly-opened grave and thick enough to muffle the cries of a whore being disembowelled near Whitechapel. Marc, my new time-keeper on earth, had just turned two, so it was 1974 when I left him with our Irish au pair, Annie, and set out for the local shops on foot late one November afternoon. The door had barely closed behind me and I had taken a few steps, not quite as far as the front gate, when suddenly every familiar thing one counts upon simply vanished. Where was the front gate? Where was the house containing a beloved child, the lime trees, the pavement underfoot, the rubbish bin? Damn. Where was my hand in front of my face? I inched along until the curb where Ellingham Road met Percy Road was sharp under the arch of my foot. It was impossible to see or hear if traffic was approaching. I felt my bearings start to go adrift in the mucous fog that blinded me and filled my lungs. I had become a ghost, naked and invisible, there and not there, with hardly more than a memory of what solid life was all about. Up and down were escaping me too, and I was feeling myself turning slowly like a soggy pinwheel when a cheery bell sounded right at my elbow. There, inches away, greenish mist clinging to his helmet, was our local bobby on his push-bike.

'Evenin', Miss,' he said.

'Good evening, Constable,' I replied, with a shiver of thanksgiving for the comfort of his presence, and also because any kid from Jersey City who loves old movies and Sherlock Holmes has dreamed of the chance, if only once in this life, to hear herself say: 'Good evening, Constable.'

'Thick one,' he said, brushing his cape where the fog had condensed into droplets.

'It is,' I said.

'You'd better get yourself home, Miss. Be all right, will you?'

'Oh yes, I think so,' I replied. 'Constable.'

'Well, I'll be off, then,' he said.

He touched the brim of his helmet and disappeared. The bell on his bicycle rang as distantly, say, as a costermonger's sing-song in Lambeth Walk before it was swallowed up and carried away by the last great London fog.

Lillian's mother passed away on the great fog of 74, and Oberon, the dog who lived to hate, died not long afterwards. After a suitable period of mourning, Lil bought another west highland terrier pup called 'Jackpot' and raised him to be the most sweet-tempered of dogs. Finally the day came when with the hopes and hungers of a long-term prisoner reprieved, Lil left England to live out her dream of expatriation in France. When the property she and Chris moved into near Beauvais turned out to need more work than they could afford, Lillian devised an insurance diddle, something to do with the disappearance of one of their cars; the scam went haywire thanks to Chris who was too honest and funked it. While he was in London for a few days 'R&R' after a near escape from French justice, he established what was to be an enduring relationship with a bel canto tenor from Texas, and when Lillian found out she was as heartbroken as any conventional wife. For weeks she rang me every night from France, sometimes weeping in her smallest voice like a lost child; later on, booming: how dared he, after all she'd done for him? Finally she sold up at a loss and moved to Paris and a job on the Champs-Elysées in the French office of an English news agency. Eventually she and Chris made a shifting truce, but she started gaining weight again and whenever I saw her after that, in Paris or London, she was always a little bigger than the time before.

Meanwhile Lil's phone calls were not the only ones I had begun to receive from troubled friends, and friends of friends, and errant neurotics passing through London from all over the English-speaking world. My own emotional troubles were not behind me: I hadn't yet undertaken the primary acts of forgiveness, for instance, with which wisdom begins, and I was within a decade or so of retirement from my own romantic skirmishes. For some peculiar reason, as far back as I can remember, other people's troubles have interested me deeply and unsentimentally; I understand them better than my own and I see through them so easily that it never entered my mind that the white witch facility, or the tact of the Rabbi's wife, or whatever you choose to call my mix of common sense and intuition, wasn't universal among my sex. I thought all women had distaff smarts – we certainly all believe we have it – until the day came when I myself sought the advice of a female friend or two, and found it to be egocentric, judgemental, and really, really bad.

'Buy a car,' Donald said, exasperated one night at my place after a series of long conversations with weepy callers had prevented me from finishing my dinner. 'I'll get you a sticker for the window that says: "Agony aunt on call"!'

By that time, I had proven myself not comfortable on television; not as learned, decided, or po-faced as contributors need to be for weighty journals of the right or left; and not well enough versed in the local idiom for down-market media which, anyhow, bores me. When it came to print journalism, I was damn near useless in fact: I have always admired books too much to review them; I love the theatre but never come late; and to tell the truth, by the time *Nova* died I had interviewed enough celebrities to know how few of them were even as interesting as I was. With the best will in the world, what was London to do with me? In my memory, the dear old city breathes a sigh of relief when in 1972, Deirdre McSharry, editor of the brand new British version of *Cosmopolitan*, asked if I'd like to write their agony column and because I have always been profoundly nosy about other people's private lives, I said 'And how!' A niche had been found at last for the Yankee who simply would not go home. I've been an agony aunt for more than twenty years in four English-speaking countries, and the single reason I've lasted so long in the role is that even though God knows the job has upset me, infuriated me and depressed me, not for one moment has it ever bored me. 'Agony aunt': it doesn't sound like much of an occupation for a grown woman, does it? If I had stayed in New York, channelled my wanderlust and sublimated my curiosity, the world would probably have had to contend with yet another lady novelist. But nobody invited me to London and nobody asked me to hang around; 'agony aunt' is the best London can do for me and it isn't bad at all. In fact I've been a busybody since the day I was born and it was about time someone paid for what I'd been handing out free all my life.

Fifteen years on, Ellingham Road represented the flat of my life when the usual emotional highs and lows were contained within parameters of devotion and duty. The way single mothers used to make paper-flowers until dawn to keep their little households afloat? That's how I churned out freelance journalism: six or seven pieces a month over the Agony Column to pay mortgage, taxes, school fees and keep us going in comfort. Even with plenty of work, my finances have been a lifelong juggling act. When I wasn't making money, I went into homemaking in a big way. I spent a lot of the 1970s abroad in the fabled land of contentment and fulfilled women, where like any other tourist, I stinted on sleep and ran around frantically sampling as many local attractions as I could before it was time to leave. I pickled herrings, eggs and onions; I baked Christmas cakes, birthday cakes and hot-cross buns in season, made steak and kidney puddings and shepherds pies from scratch, taught myself Indian cuisine maharajah style, stewed chutney out of the small hard pears that dropped into our garden from the tree next door; I grew lemon thyme, dill, tomatoes, delphiniums and roses. Marc's nursery-school friends were invited to his birthday parties; I nagged him to practise the piano and later the French horn – naturally, he abandoned both instruments in due course for a seducer's guitar – and sometimes I surprised myself in communion with local women over the merits of cleaning agents. Friends dropped in practically every weekend and brought friends of their own; people were always staying the night, emerging from the spare room on Sunday morning or rising up out of cushions in corners of the living-room. Visitors seemed to be drawn through the front-door and straight downstairs to the kitchen; some 'regulars' to the house hardly knew there was a living-room upstairs, or any chair other than those around the kitchen table.

My kitchen had been paid for with the ill-gotten gains of ghostwriting a book about Saudi Arabia, where I had never been. The putative author was a German spinster of my own age, a self-absorbed traveller who had taken in so little of the colour and pace and habits of the place during her years there that I, in effect, invented Saudi Arabia for her book. When the cursed job was finished – just in time, one more hour of her wheedling Teutonic enthusiasms would have finished me – she gave me a horrible necklace set with teeth drawn from deer her father used to shoot for sport, or so she said, set in dental-looking gold. The walls of the kitchen her book bought me were the colour of Superman's tights, skirting boards and trim were black and a bright yellow table sat in the middle of the room with four yellow chairs. For the very reason that earning the money that paid for the kitchen had been so hard and unfunny, I wanted to make it look primary and fun, like a cartoon strip. Kitchen conversations were uproarious, honest, intense, occasionally erudite, sometimes uplifting, usually boozy, often stoned, never dull. Nor ever in fifteen years did anyone walk out in a huff any further than through the back-door into the garden, whence he – more likely it was a she – soon came back holding out an empty glass for wine. It wasn't so much a salon that met regularly around my yellow table, it was more a kind of saloon.

Marc grew of an age to need a chauffeur as much as a mother, and au pair girls became a regular feature of life at Ellingham Road. It was a cushy job, and as soon as one girl's term was up, candidates were queuing at the door hoping to install themselves. My little household was not so relaxed as a youngster might mistakenly believe upon seeing the empty wine bottles and eccentric guests; it functioned strictly according to my rules, and rules were adjusted only to my son's needs. I was running an Englishman's home after all, and to hire the wrong au pair was like introducing dry rot into a castle. The girls were all students in London to learn English, none of them had references outside their own families, and I chose them pretty much on intuition. Twice, trying to be trendy, I hired boys and those were the times I went wrong. Otherwise even the silliest of the girls took to nursery routine as an extension of playing with dolls, and I never caught a girl eating three out of four fish-fingers on the plate before the baby even had his bib on. Admittedly the girl from Bilbao arrived pregnant by a married man at home, and one of the provincial French girls fell madly in love with a gypsy boy she used to bring back from an encampment under Westway. He gave my son his first case of head-lice. (It could have been worse.) Ingrid, a willowy blonde Swede, and our last au pair, was pleasant enough and attentive to Marc and me; she couldn't help it that she preferred the cat Merton to either of us.

'The Bertrand Russell of cats,' Don-Don used to say, stroking Merton's ears.

Once past Shepherd's Bush Green, Don-Don claimed he needed a dragoman, and he rarely came to visit me at home. What did he know about putting up day in and day out with a cringing feline failure whose hungers stripped him of dignity and kept him perpetually hanging around my ankles, like shackles? I loathed that cat. Tony almost persuaded me it was because Merton had been his studio cat; but the truth was I'd not taken to the beast from the first time I'd seen him, a fishy-looking kitten with a coat that was layered like scales. Merton and I were temperamentally unsuited. My favourite was our tortoiseshell, 'Janet Goldberg', whom we had rescued as a kitten from the street. Now there was a cat who knew when to purr and when to shut her gob; she walked in pride not trying to ingratiate herself with the boss like a furry four-footed Uriah Heep. Marc loved Merton, of course, preferring him to Ingrid, or any other of our au pairs, except pretty little Moy from Thailand. Oh yes indeed, there was a strong element of situation comedy about our home back then: sit-coms are epic sagas in the land of cottages and cats and birthday cakes.

Certainly Ellingham Road was not how I would have said a life in London was going to turn out. Of all great cities however, only in London could one lead a life of rural domesticity – mine was rather a shaggy version, I admit – while twenty minutes down the road were seedy bars crawling with writers, and restaurants, and seats available for the best theatre in the western world. The secret of London's laid back nature is in the garden. These British Islands sit like a flotilla surrounded by ocean, and on a good day, Londoners' gardens are open to every sea-bright breeze. From early April, no matter how congested and difficult the day ahead was going to be, I began it peacefully like countless other Londoners, out in my own little garden, cup of tea in hand, seeing what was sprouting, what was blooming, and for a few minutes taking to heart life's gentle goodness in spite of bills and the rat-race. The day ended with equal calm on the long shank of a northern summer evening when we Londoners sipped white wine in our gardens and listened to the branches rustle like rigging in the wind. London gardens are not set out like front gardens in provincial France, as neatly as a bourgeois dinner-table. Small though the London garden generally is, it is woody and romantic, evergreen, overgrown, tending to shade, and hidden from the neighbours by leafy walls. Austere nautical solitude combines in it with the velvety clutter of a Victorian parlour. Stone cats, urns and statuary, sunken bathtubs converted into ponds, miniature pagodas, small grottoes: I've never seen a London garden that lacked a touch of folly. During the philistine 1980s, when the government's ruthless pursuit of the trite and ugly prompted them to replace the dear red telephone-boxes with something banal, someone told me where I could buy one of them for £200. I thought it would look splendid in the far corner of our garden. That my folly was not to be in the end except in my imagination, doesn't mean that now whenever I remember my garden I don't still see the old red box, overhung by the elderberry tree next door, set up over the remains of a bomb shelter where nothing much would grow, wired for light and ready to beam in Sherlock Holmes out of a pea-soup fog. Although the phone box turned out to be impracticable I did have a zany feature in my garden that was more a prank than a folly: I used to salt it with rocks and shells and pieces of wood brought back from journeys to foreign places. Naturally I chose my relics with attention to how they looked, but my purpose was mainly to make mischief. Imagine a geologist of the future: a woman in the style of Raquel Welch, voluptuous and dressed in clingfilm, the way women geologists are on B movie star ships. For months she and her colleagues have been sifting through the site of ancient London, and now she has come upon a chunk of rock in what was once upon a time my garden. It interests her; she studies it with increasing excitement.

'Great Scott!' she cries. 'What is a chunk of Manhattan schist doing in the middle of a Shepherd's Bush dig? This cannot be! Clearly, we will have to revise all known theories of creation.'

Marc was seven when Hank arrived from the States in advance of his wife and their little girl, to find a place for them to rent in Spain for the summer. He dropped his suitcase in the hall and went directly up to the spare room where he wrapped himself in a quilt and took to his bed. Withdrawal from heroin was not as I had imagined: it was dead quiet, for a start, with all the melodrama of mud. Misery gathered in the spare room, it crested and rolled out thickly into the garden where I sat in a deck-chair with my head in my hands. For three days Hank had not emerged, he'd barely spoken except twice to ask for a bowl of breakfast cereal. The dank smell that came off him pervaded my house in spite of incense and open windows, and found its way into my clothes and my hair. I swear by the end of the third day his rotten cold turkey stank in my bones. Finally, it was more than I could bear; I made some phone-calls, one to a friend with a car. Hank shook and sniffled in the back-seat all the way to Harley Street and the surgery of a junkie-doctor that a friend of a friend had recommended. More eerie than withdrawal and much more alarming was the speed of Hank's recovery; within minutes of a shot – it was methadone, I think – the old Hank was back, making me laugh in spite of myself and reciting from memory sections of an epic poem he was writing. The work was published later, not quite privately, and admired by a number of critics, including Don-Don who called it a work of genius.

If my chronology regarding Hank is particularly shaky, that's because he succeeded for a while in travelling outside time. At some point he and his wife lived in London; I used to see them off and on. Their daughter was born here. She was a healthy, pretty baby, so I guess Hank's wife laid off the junk while she was pregnant. Between birthing and addiction, Hank's ménage certainly made the most of my National Health contributions. Their little girl was two years younger than Marc, and when she was four or so they moved back to the States. Next thing I heard, Hank was teaching at a western university, I can't recall what subject, something raw and flowery: Anglo-Saxon I think. Even in America he remained an expatriate, for he was travelling in junk which is a nomadic nation on this planet. He didn't need to tell me, for I knew his attraction to rock-bottom, that he and his wife were sharing needles with California riff-raff. It was a few years after his attempted withdrawal in the spare room before he turned up again to stay a few days in Ellingham Road. Except for Marc, asleep upstairs, Hank and I were alone. Earlier we had nearly quarrelled when he laughed at me for saying that joy could be a wellspring of creative genius. What was going to be my last love affair was on the rocks and I had the blues, so I dropped my arguments and let him rip on about François Villon, Dostoevsky, art under sentence of execution, Sade, Céline, Wagner's iron-age *Ring*, Baudelaire in a bad mood, foot-tapping death, despair and sodomy – Burroughs was small potatoes in the catalogue. I let my mind wander for a minute or two; it was Hank's abrupt silence that brought me back. I looked over to where he'd been sitting: he was no longer there. I had smoked pot in my day and taken LSD twelve times – 'trips without a passport', Donald called those strange journeys from which the traveller brings back illegal souvenirs – but that was kid's stuff. A dangerous stranger was glittering at me from the wing-backed chair near the fire, a desperado in whom more than childhood had ended: the future was not there, the present was starving – it was all over. The last of our good days and our old camaraderie on the road had vanished down the drain into bacterial lusts and destruction. That night I took my sleepy child into bed with me and lay awake. In the morning I asked Hank to leave.

'You are no longer ill,' I said. 'You have become the disease.'

He nodded, and he packed. Later I found a beautiful letter of love and apology slipped under my study door. It wasn't the last time I saw Hank. It was the last time I saw that other one.

The final months of my pregnancy in 1972 coincided with national strikes in Britain. National strikes remained a novel adventure for an American expat like me, even after Paris where they'd occurred, to be sure, but with less effect on my life simply because I had less of a life. Although major strikes were forecast well in advance, they arose like a force of nature, the way tornadoes do in the American mid-west say, and their impact always came as a surprise. In Ellingham Road we shared candles during the strikes, exchanged opinions and raised money for needy strikers so they could continue what even the lonesome Tory voters on our street felt on a level deeper than politics to be the ongoing human struggle against overlords. Lacking electricity, transport, gas and other amenities without which most Americans don't know it is possible to survive, we all went back for a while to old-fashioned ways of doing things. Somewhere in a junk shop I'd found a pianola with about fifty rolls of music, and I spent a lot of time while the electricity was down pumping the treadmill, making the keys skip to old marches and ditties from operettas and the music-hall. One gloomy afternoon in early August when rain was threatening, I pumped on the piano, singing along: '. . . all those endearing young charms . . . like fairy gifts, fading away . . .', when a nasal tenor voice from the street called out: 'Oi! Oi! . . . Bring . . . Bring . . . Bring!'

Clouds had been gathering and the sky was dark grey behind the leaf-green of the lime trees, a combination of colours that always tries to return me to a forgotten moment in childhood. The stranger at the door, I'm sorry to say, reminded me of our cat Merton: abject I mean, and shrewd as a monkey. He was around 40, small, wearing a shabby old Burberry that was too heavy for the season and much too big for him.

'I'm Reggie Self,' he said, 'the knife-grinder, see?'

His whetstone was on a treadle in the back of his van. Sparks flew from the knives I gave him, thunder was rolling in the distance and down the road at their gates stood the fireman's wife, the old woman with a bomb in her attic, Richie's mum and the fat woman at number 20 who was no better than she should be, all waiting with knives and scissors.

Every six months or so Reggie came by, calling 'Oi . . . Oi . . . knives and scissors, scissors and knives . . .' One cloudy day in the summer of 1982 when Marc was nine, the trees were waving over the miniature Victorian town houses of Ellingham Road, and Reggie hung around clutching my freshly honed cutlery. Never much of a man for talk, he clearly had something on his mind.

'Will you lend me a tenner, Ma'am?" he asked at last. 'There's no future in knife-grinding and I need a new suit for a job. I'll pay you back in a fortnight, God is my witness.'

I wonder if anyone else gave him a tenner? The arty daughter of a lord had recently moved into the house to the right of ours, I'll bet she gave him ten quid, too. And so did the surgeon from Charing Cross Hospital, probably. He'd bought the house to our left after the old man who'd lived there since 1918 died in the upstairs bedroom. There was a minor pop-star who had moved in across the street; I'll bet he was a soft touch. In any case, Reggie Self never paid us back. Not he, nor any other knife-grinder, was ever seen again in Ellingham Road.

14

Crouch End

Not long ago I watched while a Frenchman in his late forties regaled a bar full of his compatriots with his mother's recipe for Blanquette de Veau.

'One good carrot, scraped, a single nut-sweet carrot cut in four. One good onion, only one, you understand, studded with two cloves, two cloves only, more is too many. And the veal, aaaah! It must be young, springy to the touch, just barely pink . . .'

By this time his eyes were closed and when he started to make stirring motions delicately from the wrist, 'Simmer . . . simmer . . . simmer. Never let it boil . . .', the whole room sighed and salivated. It's not hard to understand why the French make it a rule to take their main meals decently at home within the family; any passion as hot as theirs for cuisine must be controlled. Naturally they discourage clandestine or promiscuous indulgence in the pleasures of the table; when they must entertain guests, they choose to do it out in the open in a restaurant. Manhattanites on the other hand, get a kick out of inviting people over, but because most of them cook in a cupboard and eat in an alcove, it has to be for drinks or a buffet rather than a sit-down meal. In Los Angeles folks dine on Sushi, barbecue and other dishes that don't require cutlery; their dinner-parties, being often al fresco, can't work up to the hot-house intensity of London counterparts in the

1970s and 80s. Being a guest at a London sit-down dinner-party back then was as close as a guiltless woman needed to come to trial by jury by her peers and a hanging judge. The only comparably savage and incestuous gatherings I know are given by the expatriate Brit and Yank enclaves in Tuscany where to this day guests are regularly minced in the metaphor and served up to each other at table.

London dinner-parties in my crowd were strictly distaff entertainments; men by and large attended on sufferance and would infinitely rather have been at the pub. In the olden days, at sit-down dinners among the gentry, women used to retire after the meal and leave the men alone to sit around talking man-talk over port and cigars. Sexist discrimination of that nature was not for us; we were in the throes of raising feminine status, and though sometimes the menfolk met earlier in a local watering-hole then all turned up together around eight, drunk as lords, once they sat down at table, if they knew what was good for them, they did as they were told and they listened when the women were speaking. Clamorous though London women had become for liberation in general during my dinner-party years, a lot of them were at the same time unwilling to free themselves from traditional notions of how things ought to be done. Even many emancipated households, for instance, set their tables classically: man next to woman next to man next to woman next to man, who was never the bloke you'd come in with, though quite possibly he'd be the one who took you home. At the sit-down parties of one famously wilful hostess, by the time brandy was brought out – she used to call it the 'coup de grapes' – her guests were too far gone to recollect that the table they were seated around had a glass top. What could be observed going on under the transparent table-top seriously tested an expat's faith in British restraint. Not just London libido unloosed was in evidence by the end of most dinner-parties; when Londoners sat down together at table, daggers were not left at the door, and none was drawn more pointedly than by the hostess if her consort wasn't quick enough off the mark to pour, carve, pass, fetch or change a topic of conversation at his end of the table which was beneath the house standards. Old timers still talk about the party given by a pair of celebrated journalists in Swiss Cottage when the host suddenly rose, knocking over his chair, turned on his wife who had been nagging him sotto voce to pass the green beans, and announced that he was fed up with green beans, he was fed up with her, he was fed up with his whole futile, money-grubbing life and he was off to live on the Island of Kos with a red-headed graduate student from the LSE.

Food was pretty good. Most Englishwomen in those days were cooking to a higher standard than their mothers' generation could have imagined. One or two were known for cooking affectedly below the level of a greasy spoon to demonstrate how cerebral and above the kitchen were their concerns. In my set of not-so-young-as-we-used-to-be bohemians and hacking scribblers the dinner-party often had a phony feel to it, like a stab at life as the hostess imagined it in a better class with nicer ways to cook cauliflower than her own. Sometimes, for our hostesses being mostly childless were still resident in their own nurseries, dinner out in London was like being at a dolls' tea-party given by a six-year-old autocrat. Polemic was the only acceptable mode of table-talk orchestrated by the woman in the chair who, at her worst, could turn the proceedings into a parody of an Oxbridge high table. (Beware! O hands that feed me!) Debate was instigated by the boss and it could also be brutally curtailed by her: 'You will not discuss impotence!' one dominatrix shouted down her dining-room in West Hampstead: 'Not at my table!'

Of course, London dinner-parties rarely ended happily, they weren't supposed to; a successful one kept phone lines humming for the week ahead. Someone had to lose her rag, or his, otherwise the night was reckoned a failure; better yet if a woman burst into tears, and best of all, should a man be left weeping at the table while the others adjourned to the living-room to drink some more and analyse his case. Even though the same few dozen people circulated through each other's dinner-parties, and in spite of everyone knowing where everyone stood on practically every issue, tempers could be teased into a blaze again by the end of the tenth bottle. If all else failed, there was usually a drop of new blood in the mix, thanks to the recent or casual lovers of regulars, who could be quizzed on their politics, morals and taste, until inevitably a view was expressed contrary to the one endorsed by the house, and all hell broke loose. The political responsibility of a poet laureate, euthanasia, absent friends, nylon lingerie, Habitat's egg-cups, smoking as a more stubborn addiction than heroin: I have attended London dinner-parties in my time where topics as disparate as these ended in emotional violence. At the very least a guest could always be caught in the spare room on the coats in flagrant delight with another guest's beloved.

Crouch End is derived from the Latin 'crux' meaning 'crossroads', a perfectly named venue for the occasion of what was going to be my last ever London sit-down dinner-party. In March 1985, Crouch End, N6, with its Victorian terraces and several buildings of outstanding architectural value was opening up to nouveau yuppies, the way Islington had earlier and Stoke Newington was going to in the 90s. My hostess was a minor TV presenter whom I had met on one of my masochistic forays into afternoon television; her husband was a producer in the same business. When she rang to invite me to dinner she named the other guests. This was a regular practice of London hostesses; it allowed calumnies to start being spread before the dinner, as they were bound to be afterwards. When I hesitated about joining a crowd of TV people I didn't know, she coaxed me on the fashionable grounds of 'making new contacts'. In the 1980s, faced with the spellbinding prospect of 'making new contacts', it always fled my mind that I had never, not even once, been given work or made a penny out of anyone I'd met at a book-launch, private view, stand-up drinks party or sit-down dinner-party. Alone I entered the Crouch End living-room where the others were already gathered. The moment I saw the pale thin man frowning at me from near the fireplace I knew he had been dragged out of his closet for the night to be my opposite number at table, and to all intents and purposes I was on my own: no champion, no defender in the tight corner. In case I didn't know on which side bread was buttered, each woman gave her own true knight a pat or squeeze while I was being introduced. The room was the familiar double drawing-room on the ground floor. I didn't need to be told that the dining-room was downstairs – grand or humble, the dining-room was always downstairs in open plan with the kitchen that gave out on to a garden, except in bigger, grander versions of the London house where there was a door into the garden at the end of the ground-floor hall. The couple had no children so it was a safe bet that the guest's toilet was on the first-floor landing; when that one belonged to the kids, it was usually built in under the stairwell. Either way, there was invariably a shelf of early twentieth-century novels over the loo. No, scratch that: on second thoughts, in a TV person's house, it was going to be a magazine rack on the floor containing back issues of the *New Statesman*. My Crouch End hostess had made one structural innovation to the familiar set: she'd had a wall removed at the far end of the living-room and replaced by a waist-high balustrade, so guests who drifted that way found themselves suddenly looking straight down a seven-foot drop to the floor below where the table was set for dinner.

'My husband calls it the bear-pit,' said my hostess, and a shiver went down my spine.

One of my women friends is an eminent English doctor, an expert on the treatment of cancer, who tells me that in the days of dinner-parties it happened far too often for coincidence that she was seated across from someone whose closest relative had been cured of cancer against all medical predictions, thanks to positive thinking and masses of vitamins. Like me my friend was often on her own or partnered by a handicapped male, to make matters worse she was the only one of her profession present when the table proposed, as they always did, that conventional doctors were a league of charlatans joined in a conspiracy to prevent the cure of fatal illnesses. My friend blames the conversational gang-banging of a single female guest – what we began to call 'the Crouch End Experience' – on the anxiety of women when they see an interesting available member of their sex around husbands and lovers. But when I recall the snarling faces of both sexes in the bear-pit of Crouch End, I know an atavistic tribal nerve had been set twanging and that a primitive blood-hunger had chosen me, the stranger, as a sacrifice to the goddess of bullies and patron foremother of political correctness who watched over middle-brow dinner-parties of London in the 1970s and 80s.

The soup plates had been removed. I had finessed my way past HRT, pit closures, American cop-show imports and several other conversational hazards, and I was starting to relax my guard. That was when the man next to me, only the bulge of a Filofax interrupted the drape of his high-style persona, raised the topic of crime in the city. Crime increases with inequities of opportunity and prosperity, and London in the yuppie 80s was at a point where if it did not shore up its social services, it could become another 'them' and 'us' city, built on greed and irresponsibility. Only that very morning, I told him, I had seen a worrying police report in Shepherd's Bush that showed local crime to be sharply on the increase among young black men.

'Tch-tch. How can you say that, Irma,' said the blonde documentary researcher across from me in the tone of oh-so sweet reason preferred by politicians of the day; the gooey way she said my name, like a sherbet – 'Urrr-murrr' – set my teeth on edge.

'I'm disappointed in you. Tch-tch. To hear you say crime is genetic. I mean, that is just so racist . . .'

'I didn't . . . that's not what I said . . . on the contrary.'

'You did! We heard you. We heard her, didn't we?' asked the blonde's inamorato of the table at large; he was a bulky TV producer and someone else's husband.

'I didn't . . . the police report . . .'

'Ha! Ha!' cried the hostess, candlelight twinkling on the antique diamond studs in her earlobes. 'Tory government lies!

How can you call yourself a journalist and fall for that right-wing twaddle?'

'I didn't . . .'

'I'd like to know where someone with your fascist ideas gets off writing a column in a glossy magazine,' a dark woman called from the other end of the table. I vaguely recognised her from children's television. 'You ought to be working for the National Front.'

The thin man, my nominal partner, turned his back on me and started whispering to the woman on his right.

'What I said was . . .'

'What you said,' cried my hostess, out of the uproar of voices, 'was that black people are criminals. And I do not want to hear a thing like that said at my table.'

Pointedly then they began discussing work-related gossip of which I knew nothing at all. And I left them to it before the lemon mousse was served. In the taxi home, speeding past the houses of Crouch End where 100 dining-room windows were sending up the glow of autos-da-fé downstairs, I swore I would never again attend a sit-down dinner-party in London. And I never have.

Practically every female in the London media seemed to be going in for therapy by the time the 80s rolled around, or at the very least for feminist 'consciousness raising', or Buddhism, or the whole lot. The single session of 'consciousness raising' I attended with a good friend who was into it all seemed very old-fashioned to me, indistinguishable from parent-bashing sessions and orgies of blame that were popular college dormitory entertainment in the American 1950s. Truth-telling became the vogue among the 35ish to 45ish spinsters of my crowd. We told the truth about ourselves and about other people, especially when nobody wanted to hear it. Most of all we told the truth about each other, to each other and behind each other's backs. We told the truth compulsively, we told it all the time, confidently, as if we knew it. We judged and criticised each other's motives, manners and appearance mercilessly. Some of us leapt on each other's lovers too, or reputations, and then waited nervously to see who blabbed. Oddly enough, most of us lapsed hostesses of the 70s and 80s have grown up to be good friends; at the time nobody could have called us the best of sisters. Marc was young from the mid-60s to the mid-70s and I travelled less, so I cannot know for sure if articulate women in New York were as wrapped up in themselves as my crowd in London. But wherever an expat finally calls home she is going to make herself a family out of complex strays like herself, who else? They are the only ones who need a family too. All but a few were children, and bound to remain that way. By the late 1970s all my friends were British. Though resident in their homeland, nevertheless, every last one of them had rejected their family, or been rejected by it, thus they were all more or less in the same boat as me, who was travelling free of my mother-country and fatherland. In such an inward-looking, self-absorbed society it was no surprise that Rhoda's name used to pop up a lot among people we both knew. The festering underbellies of sisterly relationships were right up her alley, and towards the end of the 70s when someone mentioned that she had set herself up as a lay analyst, what could I do but laugh? Otherwise I rarely thought about my sister American, and I cannot say I missed her. We never met at dinner-parties, so she stayed out of my way I guess; I made no special effort to stay out of hers. One dreary March morning in 1979, Marc was at school and I was scraping potatoes at the sink, thinking about a piece due the next day on sexual jealousy (yes, again!). The kitchen telephone rang and before I answered it, while I was drying my hands on my apron, I knew it was Rhoda: as a squall on the horizon must turn up overhead on the dot, obedient to wind direction and velocity, it had to be Rhoda.

'I have cancer,' she said, pretty much straight out which was not like her at all.

'Rhoda never made a clean breast of anything . . .' Hank had written in a letter to me a few years earlier; I don't recall to what he was specifically referring. But they had mendacity in common, a mythomania à deux that had been the basis of their love, and later supported the steel-cold hatred between them. In the same letter, Hank gave away something I'd not known before: every woman in Rhoda's maternal line, right down to cousins and second-cousins, had contracted cancer, and most of them were dead of it. Since Rhoda had been old enough to think, all her curiosity had been stopped cold by thoughts of dying. Death seems less and less the worst thing as one grows older and more used to the idea: to be young with death in charge, however, really is a rotten cheat. We haven't much time, but time is all we have. And Rhoda's time was spent entirely waiting for the fatal symptom. At last I understood her adamant refusal to go home again. Only very late in expatriation do local disasters strike the traveller with the heartfelt horror she felt about trouble at home when she was a kid. The day a siren in the street clangs with the urgency she remembers from childhood, that's the day her exchange of destinies is complete. Until that point when the tragedies of her adoptive city and its native fears become the traveller's own, death lives back where she first became aware of it, and she can believe herself to be practically immortal. As long as Rhoda stayed abroad, she could kid herself the American destroyer couldn't find her. I've known other superstitious expatriates like Rho who feel in their bones that the grave is always found next to the cradle. Of course they're wrong; wouldn't you know? The final accomplishment of expatriation is the exchange of one cemetery for another.

I wasn't the best of Samaritans during her travail, and I wasn't the worst. Along with conventional medicine she tried every alternative practice around: she went into regular mild trances, as recommended by one group of theorists, 'visualised' her tumour and shrank it in her mind; she drank her own urine; I used to bring her pounds of organically grown carrots which she juiced and downed by the pitcher; she became a Buddhist. And I had never known Rhoda closer to contented than she was during that period when every waking hour of her day was utterly devoted to herself and to the cure at last of what ailed her. Often, I sat with her for an hour or so in front of her heater, and she'd joke amiably, not about herself, but about others in her various therapeutic groups. She lived in Swiss Cottage in a glorious studio with a gallery running its whole length under a high ceiling. Offhandedly she mentioned that Hank's family was paying her rent. She had been painting again but not selling many canvases, only a few to therapists she knew and two or three to her former analysands – she'd given up the practice – and to the members of the Buddhist sect she'd joined. They were abstracts in primary colours; a row of them was hanging over the fireplace at the end of her studio, and so was the triptych of Christ entering Jerusalem I had discovered a million years before on a sunny day in Greece.

Even at the end, 1981, when she lay in hospital with her shaven head etched in blue dye for radiation, I could not take it in that she was dying. Her forty-sixth birthday was not far away, and mine two weeks after that: we were no chickens, okay. But we didn't die. Not yet. Hell, there was stuff left to do. One bad day she sat up propped against her pillows, screaming over and over again for her mother who had long before been taken by what Hank in letters he wrote to me called 'the crab'. Nurses and other patients turned their heads away and I found myself wanting to do the same, embarrassed not by what I was hearing: by what was missing. She did not believe she was dying: 'This can't be happening to me! this isn't happening to me!'

The truth of her finale had been wasted in rehearsals.

One of the Buddhists from her sect, a slight bespectacled young Englishman, kept nearly constant watch by her bedside. He asked me if I could sit in for him for a few hours that night so he could attend a service. Rhoda was sleeping, her mouth open, her lips white and dry. I said sure, yes, certainly, of course.

'When do you want me to turn up?' I asked him. 'I'll have to get a baby-sitter for my son.'

Rhoda opened her eyes. They were the auburn her hair used to be, and they blazed with hatred when she looked at me.

'Who needs you?' she said.

She never spoke again, not to me or to anyone. She lapsed into a coma that night and died two days later, on her birthday.

I wrote to Hank in America to let him know, and he wrote back to ask me if I'd find the Phi Beta Kappa key he had given Rhoda 30 years earlier; he'd like to have it back. But the Buddhists didn't tell me when or where she was buried and they presumably disposed of her possessions, including her paintings, the Princeton Phi Beta Kappa key, and the triptych of Christ entering Jerusalem. Hank also said he was planning a long poem of loose structure entitled, provisionally: 'A refusal to come to the bedside of my first wife, dying of cancer'.

It wasn't very long after Rhoda died that Don-Don finally became so angry with London that he went back to live in America. Lil while getting bigger and bigger was simultaneously receding into a small society of stern Parisian homosexuals. I was the last expat in London. And it wasn't long before I too started thinking about leaving. Not leaving England: good heavens, no. Why would I leave England? Tea was my morning tipple, my child was English, my bank was English, so was my shoe size, and all but one or two of my friends. I spelt favourite with a 'u' and, my dentist was an Englishman. But most city-dwellers come to a passage in life when they dream of living in the country, and none more fretfully than Londoners whose parks and gardens imitate an idyll of rural life on their small island. There was a part of me too that longed to walk alone where there was no pavement, and in winter to come home to a fireside, in summer to bowls of soft fruit from my own trees. I'd have a dog, maybe a goose, on the sort of smallholding that is feasible for a woman on her own only in the sweet green counties of England. Besides, Marc was finishing at the posh prep school in Chelsea to which I'd bused him from the Bush, and in the country he could start as a day-boy at a better school than was available to him in London. We had lived in Shepherd's Bush for nearly fifteen years; I'd paid off the mortgage. It was the height of the property boom, an estate agent valued our house at about twenty times what I'd paid for it so we ought to be able to afford a little place off the beaten track in say Dorset or Devon.

My friends warned me that I was a city girl, if I left for the hinterlands I'd be sorry. But friends have an investment in the status quo, and they were wrong. I would have been no more sorry for moving to the country then than I'm sorry now I didn't. Saintly Keith had finally taught me to drive so I could run the car we'd need for country living. Learning to drive on the roads of the inner city incidentally put a few finishing touches to my general knowledge of fellow Londoners, their tendency to meander, for example, and when I was messing up a three-point turn, Englishmen waiting to pass couldn't hide their natural drift to schadenfreude. Meanwhile Marc and I had found a school he liked. It was a boarding-school with places for day-pupils too, built on vast grounds in the heart of rolling Dorset countryside. On the long train ride back I thought of gum-boots and mud, rambling roses, a dog, views from every window, logs, wasps, burst pipes, friends down for weekends. Had I noticed, asked my son, that even though the school we liked had until recently been a single-sex establishment, it was absolutely swarming with new intakes of girls? He looked thoughtfully out of the window. Light touched the hairline scar on his upper lip where years before he'd walked into a barbed-wire fence; my heart lurched to see a soft brown down setting the space for a moustache. I was dying to hug him but there were other people in the compartment and he wouldn't have liked it.

'Mum?' he said without turning his head: 'Can we afford for me to go as a boarder?'

Three months down the line, our house was sold to a man whose first act was probably to rip out my garden. Marc was enrolled as a boarder in the Dorset school we both liked. And I'd bought a small flat in the dead centre of London.

15

Soho

Are there more homosexual men in London than in other capital cities? Britain has undoubtedly produced a large percentage of history's wittiest homosexuals, especially the literary variety, and naturally most of them sooner or later headed for London where their flippant, knowing, theatrical flair coloured the entire social scene. Lonely homosexuals in the sticks everywhere go to the big cities, not to save their lives, but for the chance to live their lives, even at risk. That's what cities are for. Of course there are no more homosexuals in London than in any other capital, it just feels that way, particularly to anyone who lives as I do now in the middle of Soho, because here was the mother lode of camp, high and low, and wherever in the world homosexuals make their scene, from Singapore to Hamburg to the downhill slopes of San Francisco, their gay and weary postures derive with more or less success from a pre-war London style.

Many years ago I was in Tangiers for some reason or other, and I found myself at a nightclub where a troupe of female impersonators from Paris was being featured: they call them 'travesties' in French. But what we in the audience saw was no travesty, it was an unabashed display of screaming vanity, fabulous costumes, great wigs, legs to kill for, and a brazen sexiness that failed to be perfectly feminine for only one reason: because it was much too absolutely sure of itself. An American not much older than twenty who happened to be next to me at the bar was literally weeping into his glass: 'Please, somebody tell me those are real women! Please, don't let them be guys . . . !'

The poor kid would not have the same problem in London. You can't live here very long without running into men dressed up as women; they're on prime-time TV comedy shows, in the classic roles of Christmas pantomimes for children, and sashaying around in sequins at clubs and pubs for audiences of mixed sexual persuasions. God alone knows how many amateur transvestites pass successfully in shops and restaurants as genuine women; the public cross-dressers of London, the professionals, are often as not big solid blokes with tugboat feet who do not expect to be taken for real, not as women. Absurdly plumed, their huge boobs induced by oestrogen or taped on for the night, every word a sour innuendo, they aren't trying to baffle desire, not the way their counterparts do in Morocco, France, Scandinavia and the Far East. They really are travesties, and most of them are sending up the uncouth frump within themselves, setting her loose like a drunken matron at a church fête. Because Soho is the heart of the entertainment district, when I go out to buy my papers early on a Sunday I sometimes pass the drag queens on their way home from work. Defrocked and tired, always alone, under the vestiges of make-up and glitter dust, they show the faces of unhappy men, henpecked from within. Certainly they are nothing like the doomed and dangerous drag queens of pre-war Berlin: anima of a nation going to hell in jackboots. I do wonder sometimes if they are not the feminine spirit of a city as threatened by vulgarity in this period of its history as it has ever been by any other peril.

No corner shops to speak of, no junk shops, not one or two pubs, not one restaurant but a hundred or so of each, no milk-bottles on the doorstep, no paper delivery, no bobby on a bike, no pride in our gardens (no gardens), few locally owned cars, and no high street: that's life in Soho. Here we enjoy none of the leafy suburban charms that distinguish life in many other parts of the

city, no river views, no ice-cream vans, no Mormons knock on our
doors to spread the word, we haven't even got a local cinema,
though a dozen first-run films are always on in Leicester Square.
To live smack in the middle of London is to live less in London.
You won't find homesick Londoners abroad longing for Soho,
even if they're bound to remember it fondly when they're
stranded in Riyadh, say, or travelling through the dry cities of
Oklahoma. I can buy handcuffs or a leather mask down the road,
sun-dried tomatoes are flown from Italy to a speciality food shop
around the corner, and a street away on the Charing Cross Road
there's a man who sells first editions. But Marc popped a button
off his coat while we were moving in, and the closest we could find
to a little local shop selling needles and cotton was the big John
Lewis department store in Oxford Street. When we step outside
our own front door in Soho, we certainly do not know by name
every face in the street, and if someone dangerous walks by, we do
not tell the Neighbourhood Watch, or even tell each other: villains
come to Soho for the same reason any tourist does, to make more
trouble for themselves than for us residents. It is the only area in
London where a New Yorker dodging traffic and the human
swarm says to herself: 'Now, *this* is what I call a city.'

There isn't an area quite like Soho in any capital that I know.
Major cities usually separate their highbrows from their low-
brows, the young from the old, rich from poor, creative from
flagrantly procreative, and they generally stow their career women
well away from the working girls; but not London. London packs
them all in as they fall, and all into the mainly Georgian buildings
of Soho: the best bookstores next door to the dirtiest, a West End
Hamlet around the corner from a street of 'Live Sex Shows', a
church ten paces from a porn palace, a school where children who
arrive with nannies join voices with the offspring of junkies
and prostitutes. Gourmet restaurants, private clubs, publishers
and film-cutting studios share premises in Soho with S&M
magazines, pimps and places that sell bondage gear. Soho is not a
city within a city: it's something in itself – a fulcrum for all the

villages, north and south of the river, that make up greater London. Multiplicity, not simply of bodies but of endeavour, gives so much density to this small area that sometimes I can feel the rest of London twirling around us like a Morris Dance on ribbons around a fixed point.

Moving from many rooms to one or two requires decisions that are particularly symbolic and salutary for a woman in her middle years. When it was time to leave my house in Ellingham Road for instance, each of the several thousand books I had collected on my shelves had to be handled and examined one by one. Would I ever need *Psychopathia Sexualis* again for reference? (Probably, more's the pity.) Was I ever again going to read *To the Lighthouse*? (Not on your nelly.) Had the collected fairy tales of the Grimm brothers become a totem I could no longer afford to drag behind me superstitiously? (Yes? No. Yes! No, no.) Our hall was lined with framed photographs I had collected of ancient school groups and pre-TV amateur theatricals, and portraits of World War One Tommies smiling on the threshold of destruction, and babies in christening dresses long since worn out by newer generations. The faces had become old friends after years of passing them on the stairs, but there was no room for memorabilia in our new flat, there was barely room for memory, and the pictures had to be returned to the junk shops from which they'd come

Not very long after I'd downsized my life, my dear friend Lillian did too. There were cases around me still to unpack in Soho when Chris rang to tell me she had died in her sleep. It has always puzzled me that a few days earlier Lil had sent her inseparable companion, the good dog Jackpot, to stay with friends in the country. If her death was as peaceful and unexpected as Chris told me in his call from Paris, then why did the police seal off her flat? She did not die intestate: she left Marc her collection of old cameras, not that he received them. Many of her bequests were crushed between the laws of London where her will was lodged, and Paris where she died. Six or seven of us flew over from London for Lillian's funeral which took place at a hideous crematorium in an industrial quarter outside the city. The domed coffin covered in wreaths sat like a blooming hillock on a reinforced table. Folding-chairs were arranged around it in a semicircle three or four rows deep, most of the seats taken by tall crop-headed women in black. Around the back of the room stood some men in smart topcoats weeping in each other's arms. A speech was made in English and one in French. Lil had travelled far from her mother country, and there was no mourner to eulogise her in Spanish. Then we all stood around for a while, the women in groups glaring at each other like small islands at war; the men in pairs, trying not to giggle or display too much arch savvy. Grunting under the weight of the coffin some workmen helped Chris and a few others carry it away; another party was waiting and it was time for us to go. Chris met me at the door; he was pale and emotion was making his face twitch.

'I know,' I said. 'It's sad. We'll miss her.'

'Yes, oh yes. But it's not that. Oh God,' he said, trying hard not to laugh. 'It's the coffin . . . the coffin won't fit through the oven door.'

Later, in the car back to Paris, he said: 'Lil would have seen the funny side.'

'Oh yes,' I said, and for the benefit of her chauvinist ghost I added: 'It's what she gets for dying in Paris. Even in scatty old London, someone would have cared enough to take measurements.'

'She'd have laughed,' he said confidently.

'Yes,' I said.

But she wouldn't have. She'd have rung me or someone that night, hurt and crying, and unable to sleep.

Life in Ellingham Road had included some of my happiest times, and it had reached its natural conclusion. The books, the hot-pot ever on the stove, au pairs, cats, the deep-freeze stocked with meals, wine delivered by the case, overnight guests, truth and jokes around the yellow table, it was over and done to satisfaction:

finished. Only the garden . . . after fifteen years the garden was still in its prime and unfinished when I had to leave it, and it remains to this day all that I miss from my time of domesticity. Window-boxes are just not the same thing, though if I turn my head a certain way on the pillow and squint at the window-box upstairs, I am transported to an oriental landscape where a spreading pine tree rises up behind a house on stilts. The tree was bought from a bonsai shop a few streets away in Chinatown and the mirror of an old compact makes a real lake, surrounded by boulders brought back in my sponge bag from a trip to the tail end of Mexico. As long as I keep my head low, the big-city view of flat roofs and water tanks is blocked by poppies and snapdragons I plant in the window-box every spring, and beyond them, on the other side of the Charing Cross Road in real space, a redbrick office building rises in steppes like the broad terraces of Aztec farmers. Sometimes a bird crosses the rectangle of visible sky, the tops of the miniature roses stir in a breeze and for an instant I shrink into the peace and solitude of my old London garden.

In the main Soho has turned out to be a much more peaceful and even solitary place for me than Ellingham Road or any other part of London ever was. Here, at the eye of the urban storm, in a space too small for more than two guests at a time, and without so much as a dining-room table, let alone a dining-room, I have at last controlled my gregarious impulses. Everywhere in the streets around me there are interesting people: the moody flower-sellers at the corner of Monmouth Street, the young women who run the designer dress shop on Wardour Street, the Australian publican, Roxie Beaujolais, Steven with the wonderful rug shop near Seven Dials; there's always a mate of mine in the local pub, and I used to have nice talks with the woman who ran the strip-club next door until she sold the business and moved back to Singapore. For a gabby American who is compelled perhaps genetically to turn every glancing contact into some kind of meaningful relationship, Soho has been a lifesaver. Before I moved to Soho I was forever relating to people who did not go home at night, or even the next day. But most of the local people I know around Old Compton Street pack up at around six or seven in the evening to do their own things. Fortunately, night-life long ago lost its glitter for me (and I for it) so there is no siren call from my neighbourhood streets after dark when they turn into a huge al fresco wing-ding that would have ruined me had I set up house here when I was young and juicy. On the other hand, the theatres are all practically on my doorstep, so what used to be a special occasion and require all sorts of expensive suburban strategies is now merely a short walk and a quick G & T in the interval.

'But how can you stand the beggars?' a friend asked me not long ago.

She lives in Hampstead Garden Suburb where the beggars are very rich and have houses as big as her own. In our Soho streets people are homeless, they are young as a rule, and most of them come not from London, but from the outer regions of the nation. They arrive in Soho where most people are looking for fun and they make us busy citizens stumble over our deepest principles right there on the doorsteps of favourite restaurants. Does one give? Or not? Do I? How much? To which one? And why not to another? No, I wouldn't round up the beggars, as some good folk suggest, and clear them to who knows where? Off Soho streets, and the streets of New York and Paris, and practically every other city in the world. We need our beggars, they are good for us, they remind us of justice. Though if I could – who wouldn't? – I'd correct the fault in us that has brought them to every great city since biblical days, right to my door in Old Compton Street, collecting a toll to bad conscience.

From practically the moment I arrived in London, and long before I came to live in Soho, it was part of my London life. Early in the 1960s, I found myself for the first time in an after-hours drinking club in Dean Street called 'The Colony Room'. Up a dark staircase between two restaurants, around the corner from a Chinese primary school, the club was in a room not much bigger than my own Soho living-room now: small, I mean, very small.

Paintings and cartoons were plastered up to the ceiling on every wall, many of them portraits of the owner, the formidable Muriel Belcher. Looking like a cross between a middle-aged Miss Whiplash and the homely kid who is also the smartest in the class, Muriel herself sat night after night on a stool at the end of the bar, keeping an eye on everything.

'Give the cunt whatever she wants,' Muriel shouted over the racket, to her barman from time to time.

I had come to London not all that long before from a country where words tended to mean but one thing at a time. A New York cop for instance, interviewed by a reporter about a murder victim, would say: 'She was shot in the left chest . . .', because when he thought 'breast', he saw something inappropriately voluptuous under the circumstances, and not nice in mixed company. Language had been a literal business in my American homeland, and it took some time for me to accustom myself to the casual English way with graphic obscenities, to say nothing of an ironical taste for metaphor in general. After a while I understood that what Muriel had in mind when she said 'cunt' had to be fanciful, or why did she apply the word along with its complementary pronoun exclusively to middle-aged men? They included some world-famous actors and painters, by the by. A few of the regulars used to whisper about how much the old harridan loved children; they said childlessness was the sole regret of her life as a lesbian. Looking at her leaning hawkishly over the bar, I took her maternal urges to be a sentimental invention of old booze-hounds. Then, a few months after Marc was born a friend from the Colony rang to say Muriel wanted me to bring him into Soho for her to see. Early one evening I left the au pair with Marc at the foot of the stairs in Dean Street and went to fetch Muriel. She brushed past me and headed right for the pram.

'You've done well, girl,' she said to me after a while, and that was that.

Years later, when Muriel died, I remembered the way she had leaned in under the hood of Marc's pram and stayed for quite a while without touching him, returning one of his earliest smiles with her own smile of loss and blessing.

I had been a camp-follower and follower of camp through university, then Greenwich Village in New York, to the Parisian Latin Quarter, and finally it was in Soho that I caught up with the tail end of bohemia.

'So they have them here, too, thank God,' I said to myself the first time I walked into the Colony Room.'

The air was so thick with smoke there was no physiological need to light a cigarette of my own. Someone was shouting, someone was crying, a balding man and a woman with platinum hair were squeezing down each other's throats on a banquette in the corner. Along the bar king-pins and queens held little courts the way Donald used to do uptown in New York, and Dylan Thomas downtown, and Hank in Paris. Thirty years on, Don-Don has retreated to the deepest American boondocks, Hank and his little family have floated out of my life into a sea of addiction or rehabilitation, one Dylan at least sings no more, but the Colony Room is still crowded most nights with old-timers, true enough, and as many sweet young romantics following the scent of dead artists they admire. In 1985 however, the very year I moved to Soho, the Groucho Club opened practically next door. From the beginning the Groucho was a swish and expensive installation, designed by its founders as a place for the literati, or at least the literate, to hang out. At first it took some of the more prosperous overlap from bohemia; writers and journalists and a few old groupies like me turned up most days for lunch, and sometimes at night we established our own little beach-heads in the bar. But the kiss of the yuppie decade was on the Groucho from its inception: it soon became a big business in its own right, ever expanding into more rooms. The food is good, American visitors especially seem to like the atmosphere, sometimes a movie star wanders in; but few of the staff these days know members by name. People no longer walk in and look around to see who is there; they walk in and wait to be seen. Actors and comics who use the place have begun disappearing into smaller bars and dining-rooms upstairs, and not many of the black-clad boys and girls to be found in the main bar of an evening are known for making anything greater than contracts, or each other.

'Soho isn't what it used to be,' old hands complain, as I guess they always have. But the fact is, it's we old hands who are never what we used to be. Ways that for 100 years or so belonged to a class of intellectual vagabond – their drunken and irregular hours, weird clothes, casual sex, drug dabbling – by the late 1960s had become the fashion for all young people, even the most ordinary, everywhere. Every great city accumulates a compost heap like Soho over the years to ferment and feed the low life of the times. The poets and painters and longhaired groupies of urban bohemia are kaput, and so are the brains; they were overgrown by a ubiquitous groin-pounding excuse for music, and places like the Groucho Club are packed with the people who make money out of it. Essentially, Soho continues to do what it always did, to nourish entertainment and invention, and to decay. And it goes on belonging to the young, only nowadays they wear nose-rings, they don't know Marxism from middle management, and they are legion.

Marc and I arrived in Soho the spring before he was due to enter boarding-school. Our new flat was so small we used to call it 'the mousehole' until real mice took us at our word; after that it became instead 'the shoe-boxes', two small rectangular rooms, one above the other, connected by an internal staircase. When Marc is at home and I come down early in the morning to make tea in the small kitchen that opens on to the living-room where he sleeps, I feel like a Lilliputian stumbling on a roomful of man-child. Most of my friends thought I was crazy to move into such a small space. But it felt right from the start, and the omens were good. Merely days after moving in we went to the Soho Fair, a summer event that takes place in a local churchyard. London's street fairs are perfect mirrors of their neighbourhoods. The one in Berkeley Square for example is very posh and formal and by invitation only, or so they tell me. Chelsea was too fragmented by the time I moved there to organise a street fair; Lansdowne Crescent was too above it all. Ellingham Road wasn't grand enough for a regular fair, though we celebrated the Queen's Jubilee with bunting and trestle-tables in the street. Ritchie's mum made scones, the fireman's wife organised a tombola and everyone came out for tea. In Soho the annual fair is jumble and jazz, and always finishes with a guest appearance by performers from a local transvestite review who serenade us – visitors, kiddies and cops – with rollicking ambiguity. There used to be a pink and blue spangled tent too, set up near the refreshment stands in which 'Madame Irma' read palms. But I gave up palmistry when the credulity of my customers started to bother me. And occasionally I was alarmed to find myself knowing more than I cared to, and more than I could rationally explain knowing, about the strangers connected to the hands I held. There are fewer familiar old faces at the fair each succeeding year as cirrhosis and lung cancer and general decay goes on thinning the ranks of bohemia. But at the very first fair Marc and I attended in Soho there were lots of friends from the Coach and Horses pub and the French Pub, and clubs like Jerry's and the Colony. I drank white wine, Marc came second in the spaghetti-eating contest which I am proud to say he went on to win the following years, and we both ate brilliantly from food stalls run by local restaurants. I was sleepy and ready for home before the raffle winners were about to be drawn.

'C'mon, mum,' my son said, pulling me back. 'You never know your luck.'

'Believe me, Marco Polo, I know my luck.'

'Listen, mum,' he said. 'I do believe they're calling our number.'

We had a choice of two weeks for two in Marbella, or £1000 in unmarked notes. We took the cash. The batty old London wizard had smiled my way again. Or perhaps it wasn't a wizard after all, perhaps it was a fairy godmother crammed into bright red

spangles singing 'I'm Only A Bird In A Gilded Cage', while she
shook the thing in our direction.

Six years after we moved into Soho I set out on the most exotic
journey of my life: I went back – back to where I had never been.
Every continent is beautiful, and I believe the one I saved for last
must be the most beautiful on the planet. From the first snow on
the great northern flat at the headland of the Mississippi down to
the springtime blush of the bayous, America is magnificent to see.
Landscapes too shaggy to clip, wild and vast, will resist the
thousand years of tillage which has gentled the European countryside and brought most of it to heel. Criss-crossing my homeland
on Greyhound buses showed me a country I never knew I'd left.
America is not the urban nation that practically everyone,
including Americans themselves, thinks it is: America is a rural
nation still attached in spirit to founders who came looking for
space and utopia. Mountains, deserts, and bountiful farms make
up a continent in which the big cities are far apart, and generally
arrived at by airplanes full of passengers who have no idea of the
kind of terrain they have flown over. Chicago, New York, Boston,
Los Angeles and the other urban centres were generally mistrusted and feared by the people who sat next to me on the buses:
grannies too old to drive, go-go dancers, young men looking for
work and trouble, drugged teenagers, a few old traditional
western liberals, materialists, bigots, black people, white people,
retired folks, every kind of American except the rich and powerful
minority. Every bus person I talked to, and I talked to every last
soul who sat next to me or crossed my path, was enclosed in
America and persuaded of its superior goodness. Being convinced
that any one place is all that good pretty much requires the relative
badness of everywhere else to be taken on faith. Everyone I talked
to showed so little knowledge or curiosity about the rest of the
world that it was as if Greyhound were servicing a planet that had
not yet invented the telescope. The only books I saw being read
during my months on the buses were Bibles and prayer books: the

American belief that it is possible to become good by looking as though one is good makes them judgemental about everything, from the use of bad language to the bad use of tobacco. Their earnest and literal approach to goodness is what distinguishes Americans more than anything else from Europeans, especially from the English, truly a charitable race who tend to give the benefit of the doubt even to blasphemers and smokers. Perhaps simply because London is the capital of a small island kingdom without room for many factions, where issues quickly become national, not regional, or perhaps because it has been damaged and made wise, the London temperament rejects fundamentalism. Absolutely everything is up for review all the time, from the monarchy to the construction of a new shopping centre in the middle of Kent. London is the centre of an obsessive British self-examination that slows material progress down for sure, while it puts a spur to justice. One of the reasons the city needs so many newspapers is precisely because so little here is taken as read.

Much of what I know is what I knew. And some of what I have loved about London is sliding inexorably into the past tense. What doesn't? Who hasn't? Eight months in America was the longest period I'd been away from London in three decades. The beauty of my homeland was indisputable. However, America requires obedience, and I'm just not cut out for it. Here, obedience is not required, only courtesy, and that comes easier to me. London, like it or not, I'll stick with you, even while you and I together become less so. And more so. Ambivalent, self-searching, diffident, handsome, tolerant, widespread, whingeing, ironical, laid-back, lazy old Smoke, I like your style. Even your food has improved and your theatrical genius sometimes makes something damn near unholy happen on stage. I've managed to accept the maddening convolutions of your crosswords and bus routes, I've learned to do without fogs and shillings and knife-grinders. Sure I daydream about starting all over again. In

Jerusalem or Anchorage, or any strange city, I look up at balconies, glimpse a courtyard through a broken door, see warm lights behind windows at night, and I imagine myself entering into the rooms of that place, learning the dialect, discovering the street-life and markets. I've even imagined a life in Buffalo. But here I am. My child was born here. And London, I am yours sincerely.